Indiana Edition
HARCOURT
Science

Harcourt School Publishers

Orlando • Boston • Dallas • Chicago • San Diego

www.harcourtschool.com

Red-eyed tree frogs live in Central and South America. They live in trees in the tropical forest in areas close to rivers. Red-eyed tree frogs eat at night. They eat crickets, moths, flies, and grasshoppers. The red eyes are important because these frogs sleep during the day. If something wakes them up, they open their eyes, and the bright red color might scare away anything that would eat them. The inside covers of this book show a closeup of the skin of the red-eyed tree frog.

For permission to reprint copyrighted material, grateful acknowledgment is made to the following sources:

Atheneum Books for Young Readers, an imprint of Simon & Schuster Children's Publishing Division: Cover illustration by Peter Parnall from *Desert Voices* by Byrd Baylor. Illustration copyright © 1981 by Peter Parnall.

Simon & Schuster Books for Young Readers, an imprint of Simon & Schuster Children's Publishing Division: Cover illustration from *Crinkleroot's Guide to Knowing the Trees* by Jim Arnosky. Copyright © 1992 by Jim Arnosky. Cover illustration from *Crinkleroot's Guide to Knowing Animal Habitats* by Jim Arnosky. Cover illustration © 1997 by Jim Arnosky.

Albert Whitman & Company: Cover illustration from *The Enormous Turnip*, retold by Kathy Parkinson. © 1986 by Kathy Parkinson.

Printed in the United States of America

ISBN 0-15-340526-0

2 3 4 5 6 7 8 9 10 048 10 09 08 07 06 05

Authors

Marjorie Slavick Frank
Former Adjunct Faculty Member
Hunter, Brooklyn, and
  Manhattan Colleges
New York, New York

Robert M. Jones
Professor of Education
University of Houston–
  Clear Lake
Houston, Texas

Gerald H. Krockover
*Professor of Earth and Atmospheric
  Science Education*
School Mathematics and
  Science Center
Purdue University
West Lafayette, Indiana

Mozell P. Lang
Science Education Consultant
Michigan Department
  of Education
Lansing, Michigan

Joyce C. McLeod
Visiting Professor
Rollins College
Winter Park, Florida

Carol J. Valenta
*Vice President—Education, Exhibits,
  and Programs*
St. Louis Science Center
St. Louis, Missouri

Barry A. Van Deman
*Program Director, Informal
  Science Education*
Arlington, Virginia

Senior Editorial Advisor

Napoleon Adebola Bryant, Jr.
Professor Emeritus of Education
Xavier University
Cincinnati, Ohio

Program Advisors

Michael J. Bell
*Assistant Professor of Early Childhood
    Education*
School of Education
West Chester University
West Chester, Pennsylvania

George W. Bright
Professor of Mathematics Education
The University of North Carolina at
    Greensboro
Greensboro, North Carolina

Pansy Cowder
Science Specialist
Tampa, Florida

Robert H. Fronk
*Head, Science/Mathematics
    Education Department*
Florida Institute of Technology
Melbourne, Florida

Bernard A. Harris, Jr.
Physician and Former Astronaut
    (STS 55—Space Shuttle *Columbia*,
    STS 63—Space Shuttle *Discovery*)
President, The Harris Foundation
Houston, Texas

Lois Harrison-Jones
*Education and Management
    Consultant*
Dallas, Texas

Kenneth R. Mechling
*Professor of Biology and
    Science Education*
Clarion University of Pennsylvania
Clarion, Pennsylvania

Nancy Roser
*Professor of Language and Literacy
    Studies*
University of Texas, Austin
Austin, Texas

Program Advisor and Activities Writer

Barbara ten Brink
Science Director
Round Rock Independent School
    District
Round Rock, Texas

Reviewers and Contributors

Sharon W. Bowers
Teacher
Kemps Landing
    Magnet School
Virginia Beach, Virginia

Kimberly Knause
Teacher
Brantner Elementary School
Cincinnati, Ohio

Beverly W. McNair
Teacher
Hollis Hand Elementary School
LaGrange, Georgia

Chester H. Melcher
*Supervisor of Curriculum and
    Instruction—Science*
Racine Unified School District
Racine, Wisconsin

Michael F. Ryan
Educational Technology Specialist
Lake County Schools
Tavares, Florida

Sharon Till
Teacher
Chattahoochee Elementary School
Cumming, Georgia

Science in Indiana Reviewers

Carey Johnson-Young
Lincoln School
Hammond, Indiana

Linda Kazragys
St. John the Baptist School
Whiting, Indiana

Science in Indiana Photo Credits:

UNIT A: 2 Misty Minar/Courtesy of Evansville Mesker Park Zoo & Botanic Garden; 3 Courtesy of Evansville Mesker Park Zoo; 4 (t) Royalty-Free/Corbis; (b) Jeff Greenberg/eStock Photo/PictureQuest.

UNIT B: 2-4 Monty Sloan/wolfphotography.com.

UNIT C: 2-3 Carrol Ritter; 4 (t) David Muench/Corbis; (b) Royalty-Free/Corbis.

UNIT D: 2-3 Children's Science & Technology Museum; 4 (t) Children's Science & Technology Museum; (b) Andre Jenny/PictureQuest.

UNIT E: 2-3 Courtesy Indianapolis Museum of Art.

UNIT F: 2 Daniel Dempster/Bruce Coleman, Inc.; 3 (c) Clifty Falls State Park; 4 (b) Daniel Dempster/Bruce Coleman, Inc.

UNIT A LIFE SCIENCE

Living Things Grow and Change

The Science in Indiana feature begins each unit.

UNIT B

LIFE SCIENCE

Homes for Living Things

UNIT C EARTH SCIENCE

Exploring Earth's Surface

UNIT D EARTH SCIENCE

Space and Weather

UNIT E · PHYSICAL SCIENCE

Exploring Matter

UNIT F   PHYSICAL SCIENCE

Energy in Motion

Investigating

This plan will help you work like a scientist.

STEP 1 — Observe and ask a question.

Which paper towel will be the strongest when wet?

STEP 2 — Form a hypothesis.

This paper towel will be the strongest because it is the thickest.

STEP 3 — Plan a fair test.

I will put each paper towel in water. Then I will put the same block on each towel to test it.

STEP 4 — Do the test.

I'll record what happens to each towel.

STEP 5 — Draw conclusions. Communicate results.

My hypothesis was correct! This paper towel was the strongest.

Investigate More

Which paper towel will hold the most water?

Using Science Skills

Observe.

Use your five senses to help you learn.

Compare.

Tell how things are alike and different.

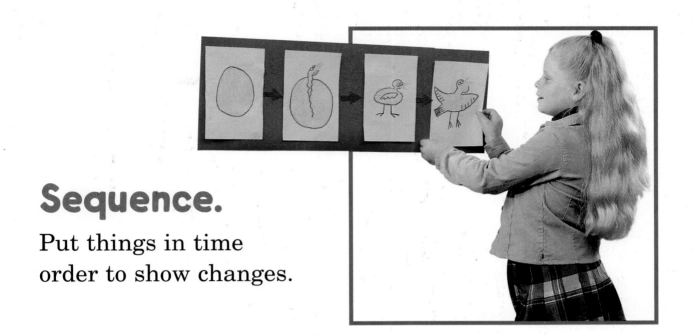

Sequence.

Put things in time order to show changes.

Classify.

Sort objects into groups to show how they are alike.

★**13**

Infer.

Use what you know to make a good guess about why something is happening.

Form a hypothesis.

Make a statement that tells what will happen. You must be able to test the statement.

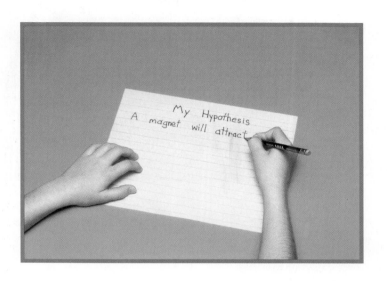

Make models.

Make something to show what a thing is like or how it works.

Measure.

Use tools to find out
how far or how much.

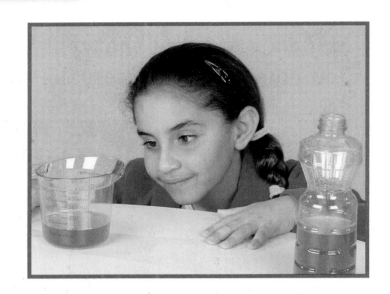

Predict.

Use what you know
to make a good
guess about what
will happen.

Draw conclusions.

Use all the information you have gathered to make decisions.

Communicate.

Share what you know by telling or showing others.

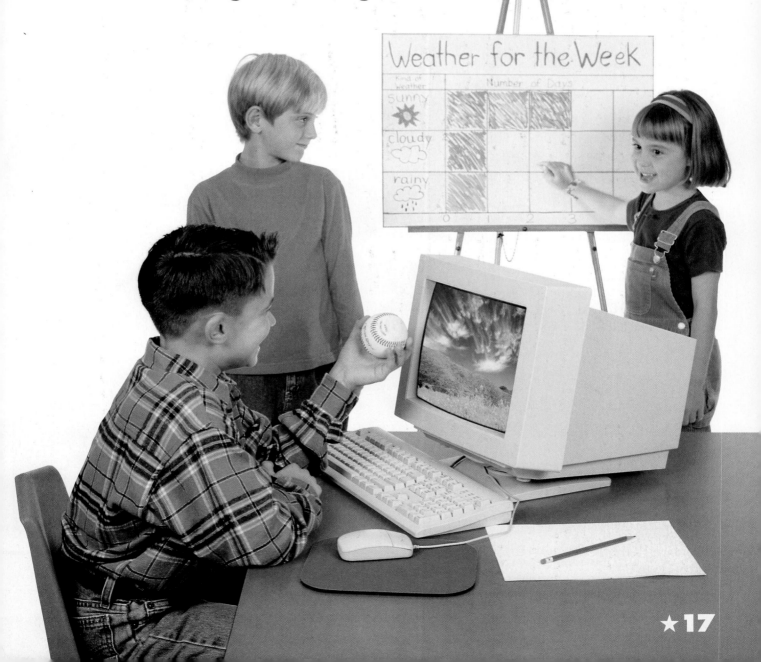

Reading

A heading tells you what a section of a lesson is about.

A topic sentence, or a main idea, tells you what a paragraph is about.

A caption helps you understand what is in a picture.

A picture helps you see what a lesson is about.

Desert Habitats

A **desert** is an environment that gets little rain. Only a few kinds of plants and animals have habitats there. Desert plants and animals do not need much water. Most desert plants store water and use it later. Many desert animals get their water from food.

■ How are these living things meeting their needs?

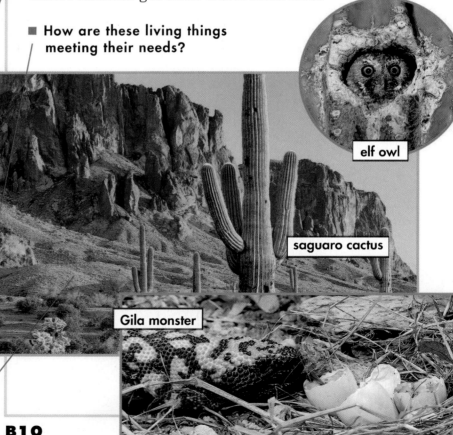

elf owl

saguaro cactus

Gila monster

B10

Rain Forest Habitats

A **rain forest** is an environment where rain falls almost every day. Most rain forests have warm weather all year round. Many plants and animals have habitats there. The plants are used as food and shelter for the animals.

■ How are these animals meeting their needs?

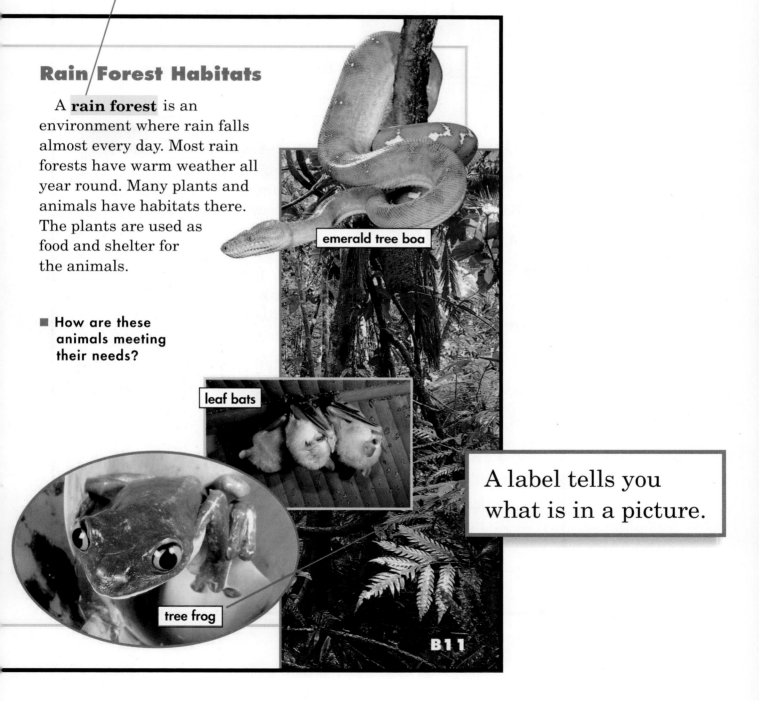

emerald tree boa

leaf bats

tree frog

B11

A label tells you what is in a picture.

A chart or table is used to help you understand information.

Hurricane

- Bring loose items inside.
- Cover windows with plywood.
- Go to a sheltered place.

A **hurricane** has strong winds, high ocean waves, and heavy rain. It can cause floods and destroy trees and buildings.

Think About It

These questions help you make sure you understand the important ideas of a lesson.

A **blizzard** is a storm with heavy snow and strong winds. It may be hard to see outside.

Blizzard

- Wear layers of clothing.
- Listen to radio warnings.
- If you can't see, follow a fence or something else you can touch.

Think About It

1. How should you dress for cold, sunny weather?
2. How are a tornado and a hurricane different?

D57

Writing

A Poem About

Poets use words to make pict
minds of their readers. These w
pictures are poems. A poet nam
Robert Louis Stevenson wrote t
poem.

Rain

The rain is raining all arou
It falls on field and tree
It rains on the umbrellas
And on the ships at se

Write

Write a poem about the kind of
weather you like best. Use the picture
in your mind to help you choose
words. Read your poem to a
classmate. Can your classmate see
the picture your poem makes?

Write

Scientists write about what they learn. They communicate results to other people. When you work like a scientist, you will do different kinds of writing. In your writing you will describe what you are learning and doing.

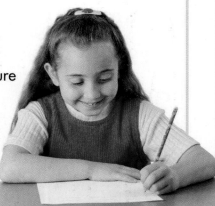

D59

Using Numbers

Scientists use numbers when they collect and show data. They must be able to understand numbers and use them to show results. To work like a scientist, you will use numbers in these ways.

Measuring

Scientists measure as they gather data. They use many kinds of measuring tools. They use thermometers, clocks, rulers, balances, and containers to measure liquids.

For more information about using measuring tools, see pages R2–R6.

Interpreting Data

Scientists collect data. Then they choose a way to communicate their data to other people. Tables, charts, and graphs are good ways to show data so the data can be interpreted by others.

You can interpret the data you read in tables, charts, and graphs.

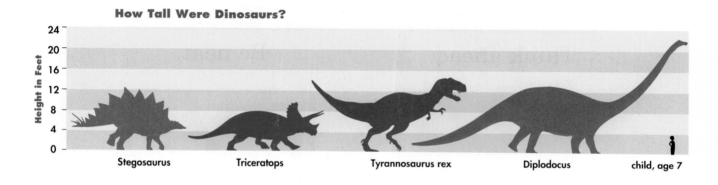

How Tall Were Dinosaurs?

Height in Feet: 24, 20, 16, 12, 8, 4, 0

Stegosaurus   Triceratops   Tyrannosaurus rex   Diplodocus   child, age 7

You can also make your own tables, charts, and graphs to communicate data you collect.

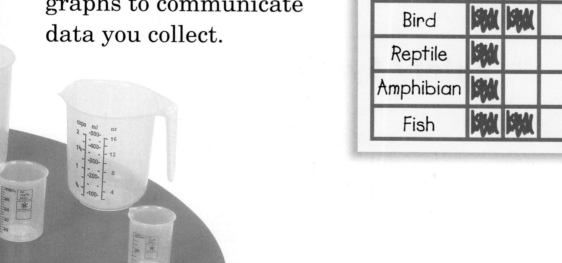

Pets					
Mammal	✗	✗	✗	✗	
Bird	✗	✗			
Reptile	✗				
Amphibian	✗				
Fish	✗	✗			

Science Safety

Think ahead.

Be neat.

Be careful.

Do not eat or drink things.

Safety Symbols

Be careful!

Sharp!

Be careful!

Wear an apron.

Wear goggles.

Science in Indiana

Living Things Grow and Change

Mesker Park Zoo

In this unit you will learn about plants and animals. At Mesker Park Zoo and Botanic Garden in Evansville, visitors observe many kinds of plants and animals from around the world.

Evansville

Mesker Park Zoo is home to more than 500 animals. There are more than 200 kinds of animals, including monkeys, tortoises, prairie dogs, and cheetahs. Two popular animals at the zoo are the otters, Splish and Splash. Visitors like to watch Splish and Splash play in their pool.

Splish and Splash

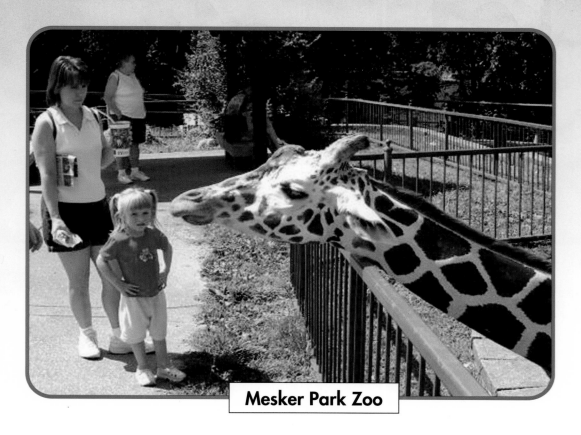

Mesker Park Zoo

We know that people and other animals are alike in some ways. They need air, water, food, and shelter. Of course, animals are very different from people, too. Their food and homes are different. They behave and communicate in different ways than people do.

People observe animals at Mesker Park Zoo. That way, they can learn about some of the many kinds of animals in the world.

Think About It

1. How are other animals different from people?
2. Why is it a good idea for people to learn about animals at the zoo?

Social Studies Link

Alike and Different

Look at yourself and a partner in a mirror. Next, look at a picture of a dog. Describe ways the three faces are alike and different. How are people more like one another than like other animals?

 Health Link

Enjoy a Hike

Hiking is good exercise. It is fun to observe plants and animals you pass on the way. With your class, hike around the schoolyard. Observe plants and animals in your part of Indiana that you may not have noticed before.

hikers

Living Things Grow and Change

UNIT EXPERIMENT

Plants and Light

As you do this unit, you will find out what a plant needs to grow. Plan and do a test to find out how light changes the way a plant grows.

Plants Grow and Change

Vocabulary

living
nonliving
nutrients
seed coat
germinate
seedling
cactus

Did You Know?
The redwood tree is the tallest **living** thing in the United States.

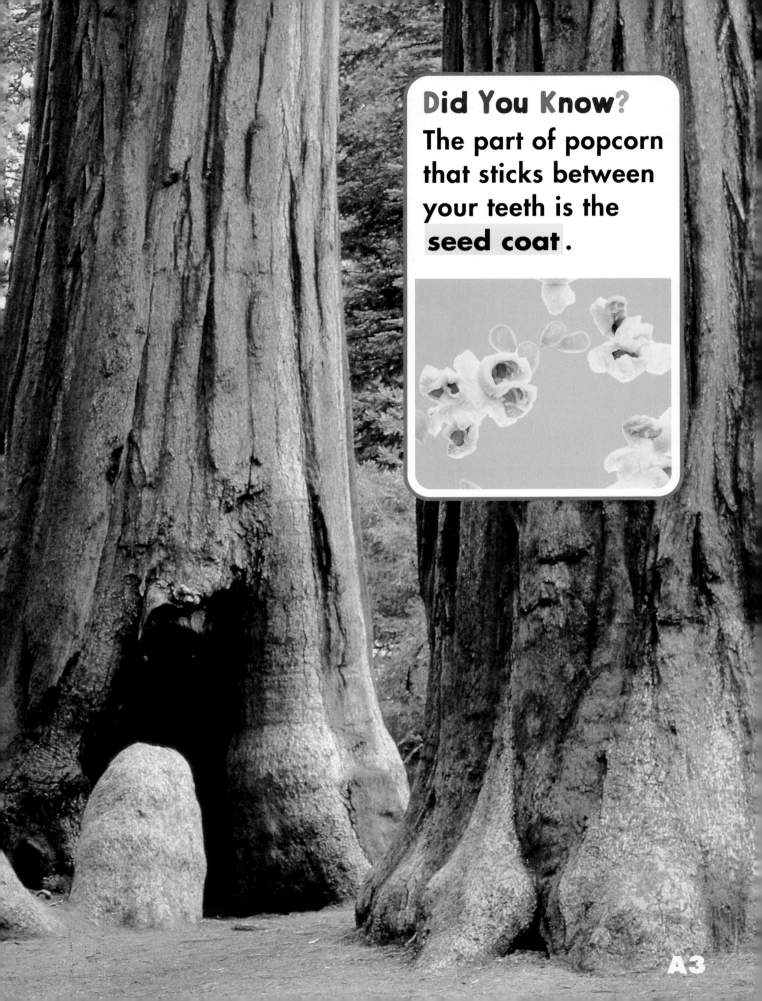

Did You Know?

The part of popcorn that sticks between your teeth is the **seed coat**.

What Are Living and Nonliving Things?

Investigate

Living and Nonliving Things

You will need

picture cards

paper and pencil

What Am I?	
Living	Nonliving

1. Make a chart like the one above.

2. Look at each picture card. Does it show a living thing or a nonliving thing?

3. Record in your chart.

4. Compare the things in the chart.

Science Skill

When you compare things, you tell how they are alike and different.

Living and Nonliving Things

The world is made up of living things and nonliving things. All **living** things grow and change. They need food, water, and air. Things that are not alive are **nonliving**. They do not need food, water, and air.

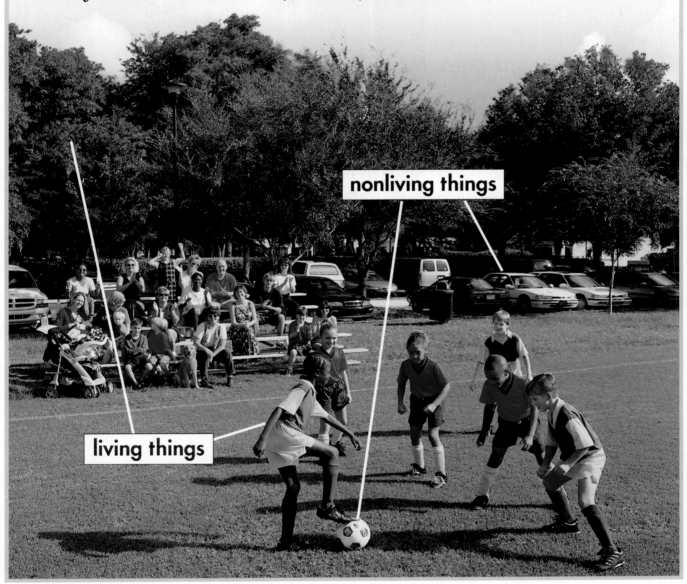

nonliving things

living things

Living Things Grow and Change

A tree and a chick are living things. They come from other living things. Like all living things, they need food, air, and water. Like all living things, they grow and change.

- How do you think the chick will change?

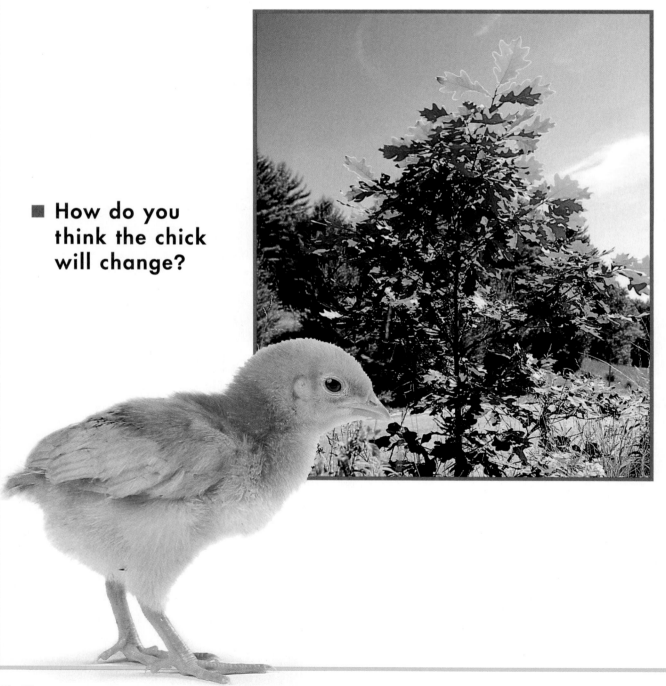

Living Things Need Nonliving Things

Air, water, and light are nonliving things. They do not grow. They do not need food.

Living things need nonliving things. Plants need air, water, and light to grow. People and animals need air, food, and water to live.

■ **What nonliving thing is this girl drinking?**

Think About It

1. What are three ways living things are alike?
2. How do living things use nonliving things?

How Do Plants Grow and Change?

Investigate

What Plants Need

You will need

2 plants

cup of water   paper and pencil

What Happens to a Plant	
Plant with Water	Plant with No Water

1 Make a chart like the one above.

2 Put both plants in a sunny place. Water the soil of only one plant. Predict what will happen.

3 Observe both plants every day. Write the date. Record any changes.

Science Skill
When you observe the plants, use your senses of sight, touch, smell, and hearing.

What the Parts of a Plant Do

A plant needs light, air, and water to grow. It also needs **nutrients**, or minerals, from soil. Each part of a plant helps the plant get what it needs. When a plant gets what it needs, it can grow and change.

Flowers make fruits that hold seeds.

Leaves use light, air, water, and nutrients to make food for the plant.

Stems hold up the plant and move water and nutrients through it.

Roots take in water and nutrients from the soil.

How Plants Grow from Seeds

Seeds have different parts. Most seeds have a covering called a **seed coat**, which protects the seed. The seed is made up of stored food and a tiny plant. The tiny plant uses the stored food when it begins to grow.

When a seed gets water and warmth, it may **germinate**, or start to grow. First the roots grow down. Then a stem grows up. The young plant is called a **seedling**.

bean seed

tiny plant

seed coat

stored food

seedling, 4 days

seedling, 15 days

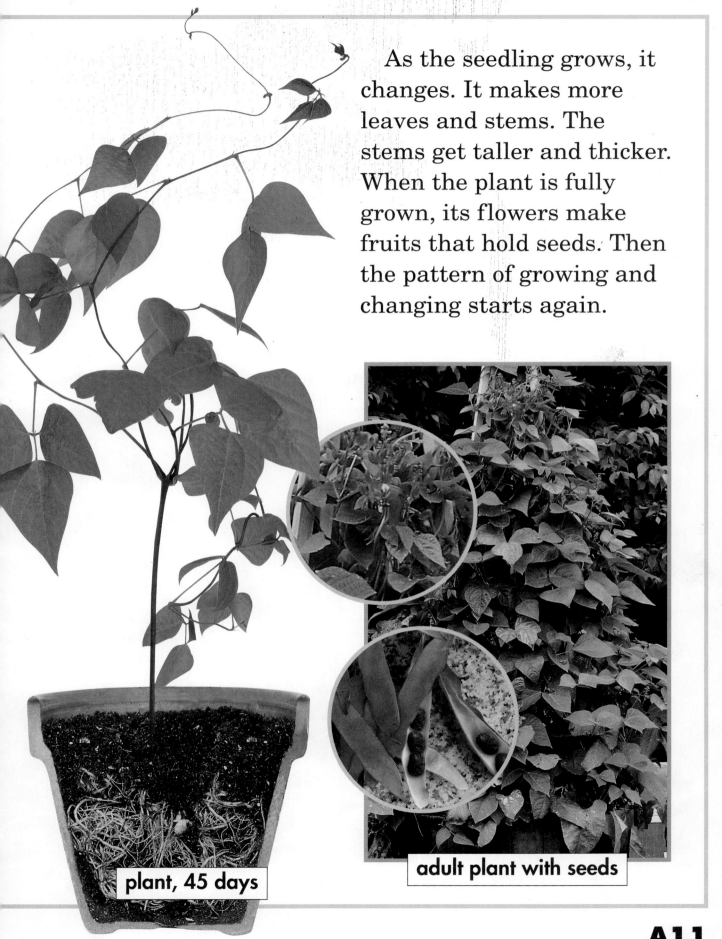

As the seedling grows, it changes. It makes more leaves and stems. The stems get taller and thicker. When the plant is fully grown, its flowers make fruits that hold seeds. Then the pattern of growing and changing starts again.

plant, 45 days

adult plant with seeds

Plants Can Change

If plants do not get what they need, they may not grow. The rain, sunlight, and even insects in a place can make the plants change. If a field does not get rain for a long time, the plants there will not get the water they need.

■ **How can you tell that these plants did not get the water they needed?**

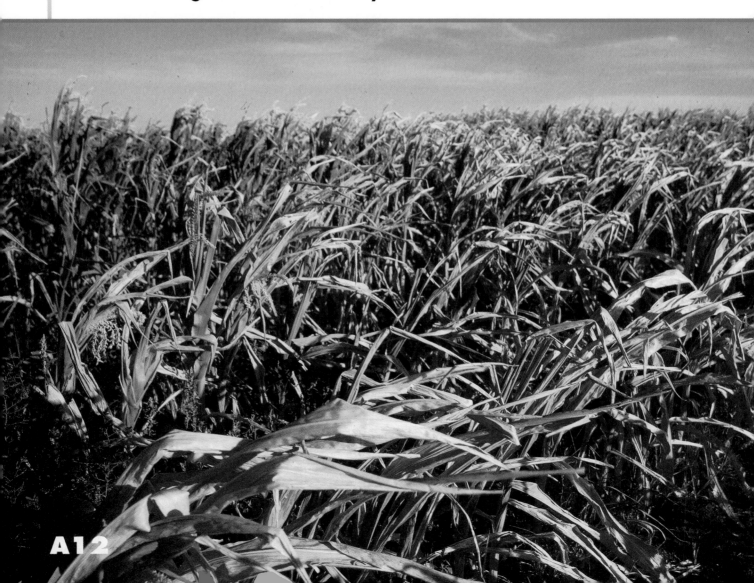

A plant needs light from all sides. If it gets light from just one side, its stems and leaves grow toward the light. This helps the plant get the light it needs to make food and grow.

■ **Why does this plant grow toward the light?**

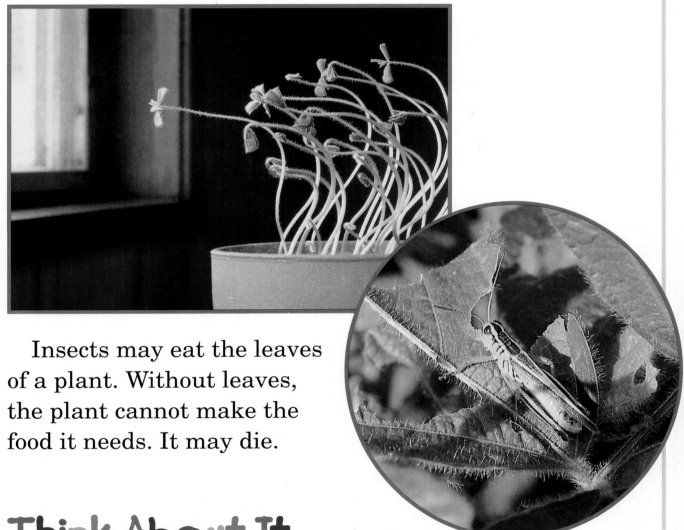

Insects may eat the leaves of a plant. Without leaves, the plant cannot make the food it needs. It may die.

Think About It

1. What happens when a seed germinates?

2. What are some ways plants may change?

How Are Plants Alike and Different?

How to Classify Leaves

You will need

leaves

index cards and pencil

1 Observe the leaves. Look for ways they are alike.

2 Classify the leaves into groups. Leaves in each group should be alike in some way.

3 Write a label for each group that tells how the leaves are alike. Tell about the leaves where you live.

Science Skill
When you classify things, you sort them into groups that show how they are alike.

Learn About

Plants in Different Places

Plants live in almost every part of the world. Different kinds of plants grow in different places.

pine forest

oak forest

desert

How Plants Are Different

A pine tree has leaves that look like needles. Its small, hard seeds grow in cones. The outside of the cone protects the seeds until they are ready to germinate.

An oak tree has leaves that are broad and flat. Oak trees grow from seeds inside acorns.

pine cone

pine seeds

acorns

■ How is an acorn different from a pine cone?

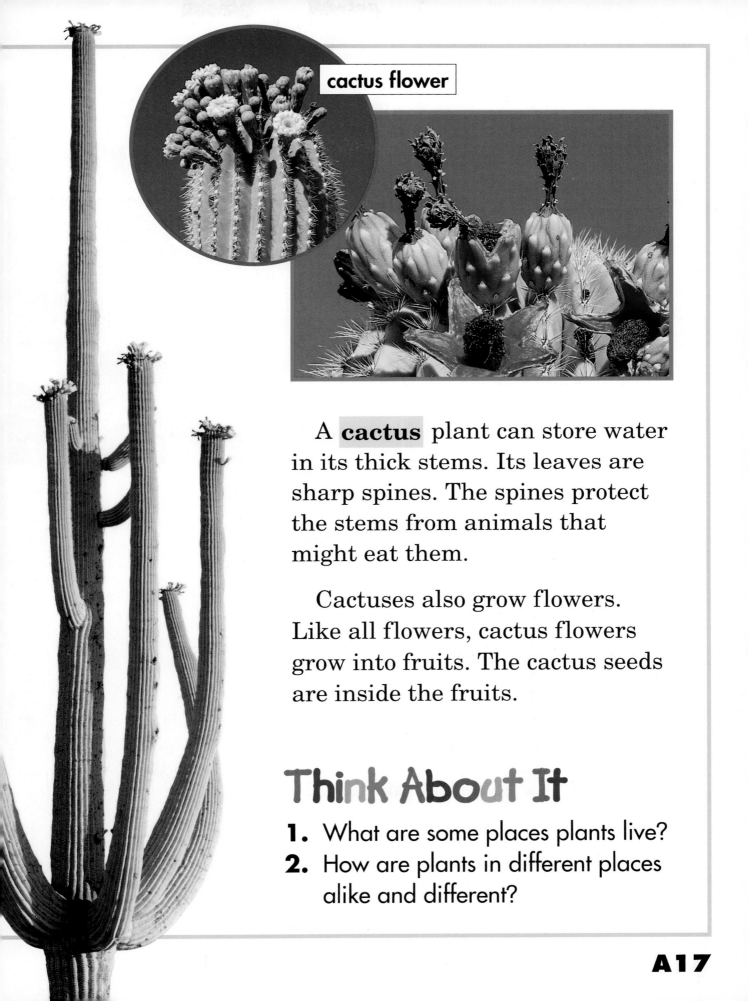

cactus flower

A **cactus** plant can store water in its thick stems. Its leaves are sharp spines. The spines protect the stems from animals that might eat them.

Cactuses also grow flowers. Like all flowers, cactus flowers grow into fruits. The cactus seeds are inside the fruits.

Think About It

1. What are some places plants live?
2. How are plants in different places alike and different?

Math Link

How Many Seeds Sprout?

Hundreds of walnuts grow on this walnut tree. A new tree could grow from each walnut. Most of the walnuts will not germinate. Animals will eat some of them. Others will not get the things they need to grow.

Think and Do

Count and record the number of seeds in an orange. Then plant the seeds. Make sure they have water and warmth. Count and record the number of seeds that germinate and grow. Write a subtraction sentence that tells how many seeds did not grow.

Jim Arnosky, Nature Writer and Artist

Jim Arnosky first worked as a naturalist. A naturalist studies plants and animals in the wild. Now he writes and illustrates children's books. In some of Jim Arnosky's books, the character Crinkleroot helps children learn about living things in nature.

Crinkleroot's GUIDE TO KNOWING THE TREES
BY JIM ARNOSKY

Crinkleroot's GUIDE TO KNOWING ANIMAL HABITATS
BY JIM ARNOSKY

Write

Draw your own character. Write a story about living things. Use your character in the story. Share your story with your classmates.

Tell What You Know

1. How are these plants alike and different?
2. How are the plants different from nonliving things?
3. How did these plants grow from seeds?

Vocabulary

Tell the term that completes the sentence.

| seedling | germinate | nutrients |
| living thing | nonliving thing |

4. Plants need water and warmth to _____ .

5. A _____ does not need food, water, and air.

6. A _____ is a young plant.

7. Plants need _____ , or minerals, from the soil.

8. A _____ grows and changes.

Using Science Skills

9. **Observe and Compare** Make a chart like this one to record what you observe about seeds. Tape seeds from different plants onto the chart. Tell what plant each seed comes from. Write your observations in the chart. Compare your observations with those of a classmate.

What I Observe About Seeds		
Seed	Plant	Observations

10. **Classify** Sort things in your classroom into groups of living things and nonliving things. List the things in each group. Tell why you put each thing in the group you did.

CHAPTER

2

Animals Grow and Change

Vocabulary

mammal

reptile

amphibian

insect

life cycle

Did You Know?
The largest **mammal** in the world is the blue whale.

Did You Know?
The walking stick is the longest **insect** in the world. It can be 13 inches long.

How Are Animals Alike and Different?

Investigate

Ways to Group Animals

You will need

animal picture cards

index cards and pencil

1 Observe the animals to see how they are alike and different.

2 Classify the animals into groups. Animals in a group should be alike somehow.

3 Write a label for each group that tells how the animals are alike.

Science Skill
When you classify animals, you put them into groups to show how the animals are alike.

Learn About

Many Kinds of Animals

Some animals have fur. Others have feathers or scales. Some animals use special body parts to fly, swim, or walk.

giraffe

tree cricket

alligator

puffin

clown fish

Animals With Bones

Animals can be grouped by their body parts. All the animals on these two pages have bones inside their bodies. They have other body parts that make them different.

Cats and dogs are mammals. A **mammal** is an animal that has fur or hair. A mother mammal makes milk and feeds it to her young.

Birds have feathers to protect their bodies. They also have wings. Most birds use their wings to fly.

blue jay

chameleon

Lizards, snakes, and turtles are reptiles. A **reptile** is an animal that is covered with scales. Its skin is rough and dry.

Frogs and toads are amphibians. An **amphibian** often has smooth, wet skin. Its skin helps it live both in water and on land.

All fish live in water. A fish uses its fins to swim and its gills to breathe.

■ **What tells you that these animals are not mammals?**

leaf frog

fish

Animals Without Bones

The animals on these two pages have no bones. They have other body parts that make them different.

Praying mantises, ants, and bees are insects. An **insect** is an animal that has three body parts and six legs. Many insects also have two or four wings. Spiders are not insects. They have eight legs.

praying mantis

golden silk spider

Worms have soft bodies. They do not use legs to walk. Instead, worms use their bodies to crawl.

Like a worm, a snail has a soft body that it uses to move. It also has a hard shell to protect it.

tiger snail

earthworm

■ **How are the worm and the snail alike and different?**

Think About It

1. What are some ways animals are alike? How are they different?
2. How can animals be grouped by their body parts?

What Are Some Animal Life Cycles?

Investigate

How Mealworms Grow and Change

You will need

mealworms

mealworm home with meal

bottle cap with water

hand lens

1. Feed your mealworms. Give them water each day.

2. Observe the mealworms every day with the hand lens.

3. Each day draw a picture of what you observe. Write the date and a sentence about changes you see.

Science Skill

You can use a hand lens to help you **observe** details.

Learn About

How Animals Grow and Change

These goslings and the lion cub are still young. They will keep growing and changing. They will grow up to look like their parents. Together, all the parts of an animal's life from birth to death make up its **life cycle**.

Canada geese

goslings

African lions

cub

How Birds Grow and Change

Birds lay eggs. First, a mother bird lays her eggs in a nest. Next, the mother or father sits on the eggs to keep them warm.

A chick grows inside each egg until it gets too big for it. Then the chick breaks the eggshell and hatches.

As the chicks grow and change, they get new feathers. They will grow up to look like their parents.

Life Cycle of a Robin

unhatched eggs in nest

adult bird

Most bird parents take care of their chicks. The parents feed and protect them until they can take care of themselves. Soon after the birds are grown, they can have chicks of their own.

chick just hatched

chick almost ready to fly

How Mammals Grow and Change

Young mammals start growing inside their mothers' bodies. The adult cat here has kittens growing inside her. When they are big enough, the kittens will be born. They will grow up and have features like their parents.

Life Cycle of a Cat

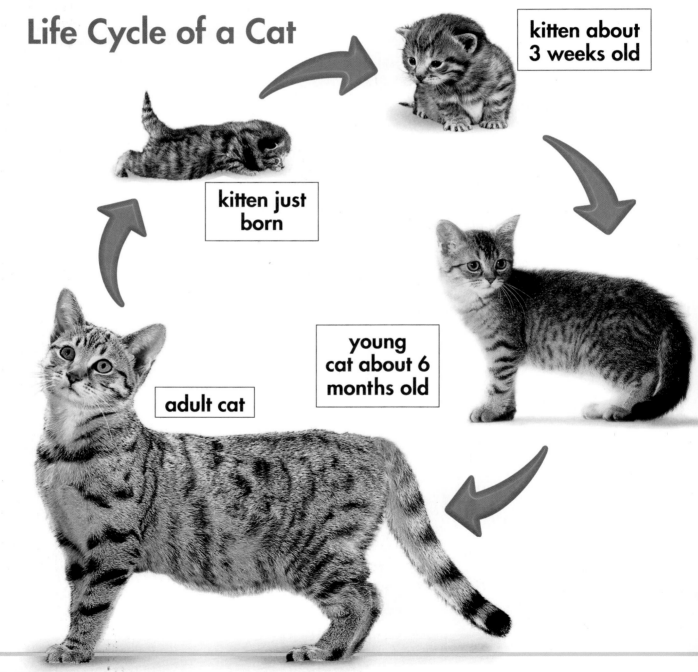

kitten about 3 weeks old

kitten just born

young cat about 6 months old

adult cat

Like other young mammals, these kittens drink milk from their mother. The milk helps the kittens grow bigger and stronger. By the time they are one year old, they are fully grown.

■ **How do the kittens look like their mother? How do they look different?**

A veterinarian is a doctor who cares for animals. This cat is going to have kittens. Why do you think the veterinarian is checking her?

Think About It

1. How do young animals change as they grow into adults?
2. What do young animals grow to look like?

Math Link

Measure Large and Small Eggs

The ostrich lays the biggest eggs. The hummingbird lays the smallest eggs. Compare the sizes of the eggs to the size of a chicken egg.

ostrich egg

chicken egg

hummingbird egg

Think and Do

The photographs show the real sizes of eggs from different birds. Use a centimeter ruler to measure the picture of each egg. Make a chart and list the kinds of eggs in order from biggest to smallest. Beside each name, write how long and wide the picture of each egg is.

Pets in Your Neighborhood

People keep many kinds of animals as pets. In many neighborhoods, people have dogs and cats. Dogs and cats are mammals. Some people have reptiles, fish, and birds.

Write

Talk to classmates or neighbors who have pets. Think about the animal group each pet belongs to. Show what you find out in a bar graph. Use the graph to write about which animal groups most of the pets belong to.

Pets

Mammal	🐾	🐾	🐾	🐾		
Bird	🐾	🐾				
Reptile	🐾					
Amphibian	🐾					
Fish	🐾	🐾				

REVIEW

Tell What You Know

1. How are these animals alike?
2. How are the animals different?
3. What is the life cycle of each animal?

Vocabulary

Tell the term that completes the sentence.

amphibian	reptile	mammal
insect	life cycle	

4. An _____ has six legs.

5. A _____ has scales that are rough and dry.

6. A _____ has fur or hair.

7. A _____ is the way an animal grows and changes.

8. An _____ has smooth, wet skin.

Using Science Skills

9. **Classify** Go for a walk outside with your class. Look for different kinds of animals. Write down the name of each one you see. What animal group does it belong to? Write the group name next to the animal name. Then tell a classmate how you know what animal group each one belongs to.

Animal	Kind
robin	bird
squirrel	mammal
bee	insect

10. **Observe** These pictures show the life cycle of a butterfly. Observe the changes from one picture to the next. Think about what you know about animal life cycles. Then use the pictures to tell what happens in a butterfly's life cycle.

CHAPTER 3

People Grow and Change

Vocabulary

permanent teeth

skeleton

muscles

heart

lungs

heart rate

digest

saliva

esophagus

stomach

Did You Know?
Your **heart** beats more than 66 times a minute.

Did You Know?
It takes 43 **muscles** to frown but only 17 muscles to smile.

How Will I Grow?

How Hands Grow and Change

You will need

paper and pencil

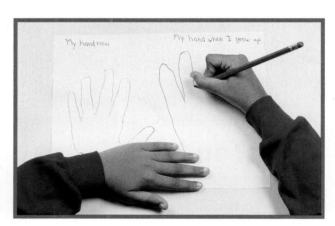

1 Trace your hand on the left side of your paper.

2 Predict what your hand will look like when you grow up. Draw a picture of it.

3 Compare the two hands. Tell how they are alike and different.

Science Skill
When you predict, you use what you know to make a good guess about what will happen.

How Your Body Grows and Changes

Your body grows and changes in many ways. You get bigger and taller. You get stronger and heavier. How has the boy in these pictures grown and changed?

Joey, 8 years old

Joey, 4 years old

Joey, 4 months old

All People Grow and Change

No two people are exactly alike, but all people grow and change. You are growing and changing. First, you were a baby. Now, you are a child. Later on, you will be a teenager. After that, you will become an adult, like your parents.

■ **Predict how the three children in this family will grow and change.**

**son
8 months**

**daughter
7 years**

**son
15 years**

When you are an adult, you will change in other ways. As you get older, your hair may turn gray or white. Your skin will get wrinkles.

mother
37 years

father
42 years

grandmother
65 years

Growing in Other Ways

Growing is more than getting bigger. You also change in other ways as you grow. When you were a baby, your first teeth grew in. Now you are losing those teeth. New adult teeth, called **permanent teeth**, are growing in to take their place.

Learning is another way you grow and change. You are changing as you learn new things.

Some things you learn can also help you exercise. Exercise such as dancing helps your body grow strong and stay healthy.

■ **How is this girl helping her body? What is she learning?**

Think About It

1. How do people grow and change?
2. How can you help yourself grow and change?

What Do My Bones and Muscles Do?

How Your Elbow Works

You will need

balloon

tape

3 rubber bands

2 paper towel tubes, each with a hole

1 Make a model elbow. Tie the tube ends together with a rubber band. Tape the rubber band in place.

2 Attach each end of the balloon to a tube, as you see here.

3 Open and close the tubes. Tell how this model is like your elbow.

Science Skill
A model of an object can show how the real object works.

A48

Your Bones and Muscles

Under your skin are hundreds of bones and muscles. Your bones and muscles work together. They help you sit, stand, walk, run, and move in many other ways.

muscles

bones

What Your Bones Do

Your bones fit together to make your **skeleton**. Your skeleton holds up your body and gives it shape.

Some bones help you move. Other bones protect parts inside your body. Your ribs protect your heart and lungs. Your skull protects your brain.

■ **Which bones help you move?**

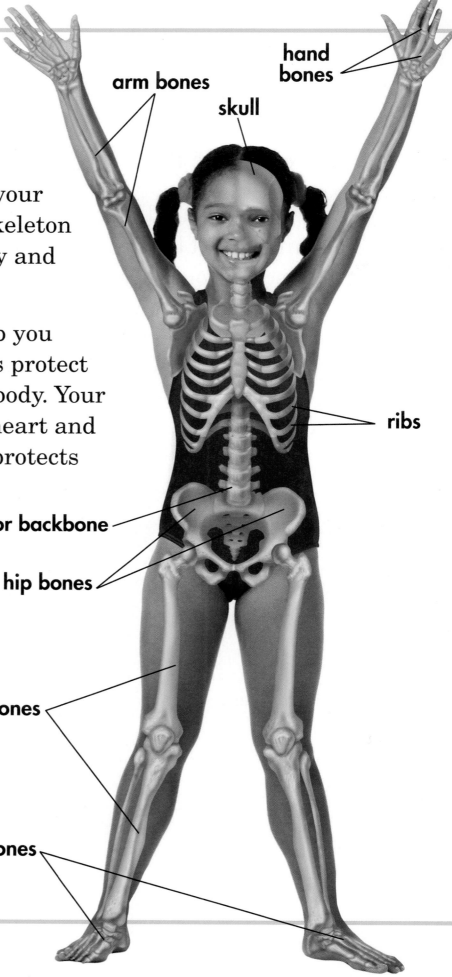

arm bones

hand bones

skull

ribs

spine, or backbone

hip bones

leg bones

foot bones

What Your Muscles Do

Your **muscles** are body parts that work to move your bones and do other jobs. Your heart is a muscle that pumps blood through your body.

arm muscles

shoulder muscles

stomach muscles

chest muscles

leg muscles

■ What muscles is the boy using to move?

Your Bones and Muscles Work Together

Muscles work in pairs to move your bones. One muscle pulls a bone to move it. Then the other muscle pulls the bone to move it back.

■ **How do this boy's muscles move his leg bones?**

Keeping Bones and Muscles Healthy

You can keep your bones and muscles strong and healthy. Exercising every day helps your bones and muscles stay strong. Eating healthful food keeps them healthy.

■ **How are these children keeping their bones and muscles strong and healthy?**

Think About It

1. How do your bones and muscles work together?
2. How can you keep your bones and muscles strong and healthy?

How Do My Heart and Lungs Work?

 Investigate

A Heartbeat

You will need

paper cup with bottom cut out

1 Work with a partner. Your partner will use the cup to listen to your heartbeat.

2 Jump up and down while your partner counts to 10.

3 Your partner will observe your heartbeat again. Is it faster or slower? Trade places.

Science Skill
When you observe, you may use tools along with your senses.

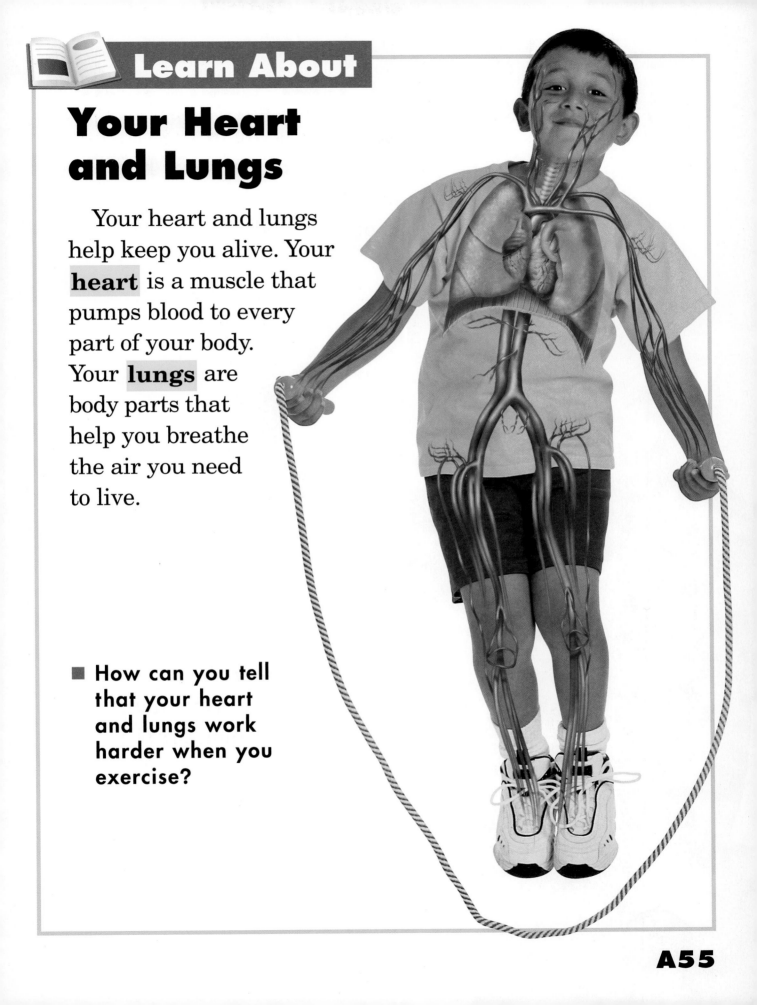

Your Heart and Lungs

Your heart and lungs help keep you alive. Your **heart** is a muscle that pumps blood to every part of your body. Your **lungs** are body parts that help you breathe the air you need to live.

■ How can you tell that your heart and lungs work harder when you exercise?

How Your Heart Works

Your heart is about the size of your fist. Each time your heart beats, it pumps blood to all the parts of your body.

Your **heart rate** is how fast or slowly your heart beats. When you exercise, your heart beats faster. Your heart rate is faster. When you rest, your heart rate is slower.

■ **In what part of your body is your heart?**

How Your Lungs Work

You have two lungs inside your chest. Air goes in and out of your lungs when you breathe. When you breathe in, the air moves down a tube into your lungs. Your lungs fill with air and get larger. When you breathe out, air leaves your lungs.

■ **Compare the inside and outside of a lung. How are they different?**

Your Heart and Lungs Work Together

Your heart and lungs work together to get your body the oxygen it needs. Your heart pumps blood first to your lungs. Your lungs take in oxygen from the air you breathe. The blood picks up the oxygen and takes it back to your heart. Then your heart pumps the blood to all parts of your body.

■ **How does blood get to your lungs? Where does it go after that?**

When the blood comes back to your heart, it is pumped to your lungs again for more oxygen.

■ **How is this boy keeping his heart and lungs healthy?**

Keeping Your Heart and Lungs Healthy

It is important to keep your heart and lungs healthy. Exercise helps your heart and lungs as well as your bones and muscles. When you exercise, your heart and lungs work harder and get stronger.

Think About It

1. How do your heart and lungs work together?
2. How can you keep your heart and lungs healthy?

How Do I Digest Food?

How Digestion Begins

You will need

cracker   mirror   paper and pencil

1 Observe the cracker. Draw it.

2 Put the cracker in your mouth. Do not chew it. Count slowly to 20.

3 Think about how the cracker feels. Use the mirror to observe it.

4 Draw what you observe. Tell what you think is happening.

Science Skill
You can use a mirror to help you observe.

How Your Body Digests Food

Healthful food has the energy and nutrients your body needs to grow and stay healthy. To get the energy and nutrients, your body must **digest**, or break down, the food.

mouth

esophagus

stomach

small intestine

large intestine

How Your Body Digests Food

Your body starts to digest food in your mouth. When you chew your food, it mixes with saliva. **Saliva** is the liquid in your mouth that begins to break down food.

When you swallow the food you have chewed, it goes down a tube. This tube to your stomach is called your **esophagus**. Muscles in the tube push the food to your stomach.

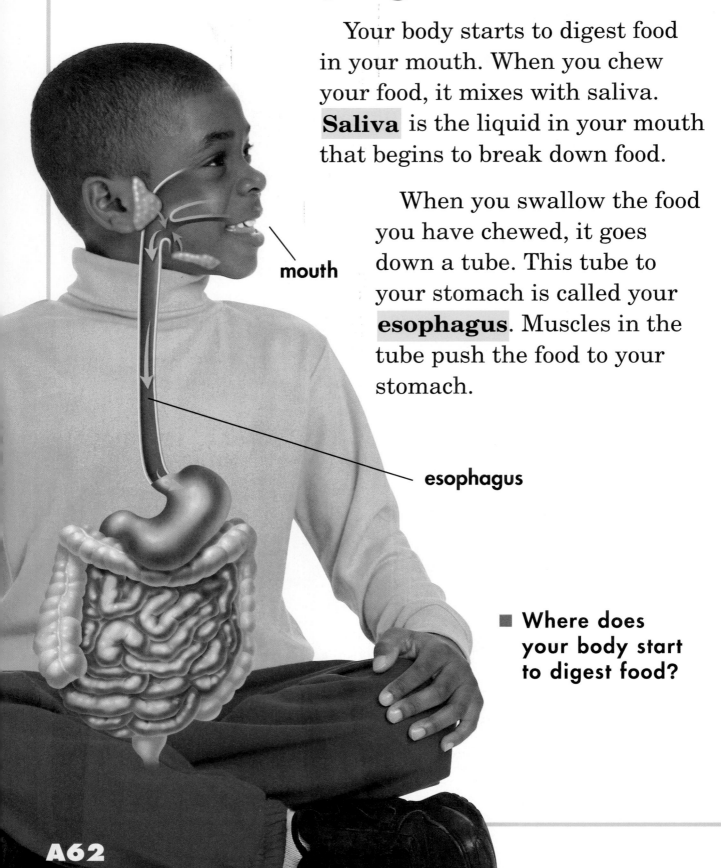

mouth

esophagus

■ **Where does your body start to digest food?**

Your **stomach** is like a bag made of muscles. The muscles squeeze the food and mix it with special juices. The food turns into a thick liquid.

The liquid food moves into your small intestine. From there, the nutrients from the food go into your blood. Your blood carries the nutrients to all parts of your body. Food parts that your body does not need move into your large intestine.

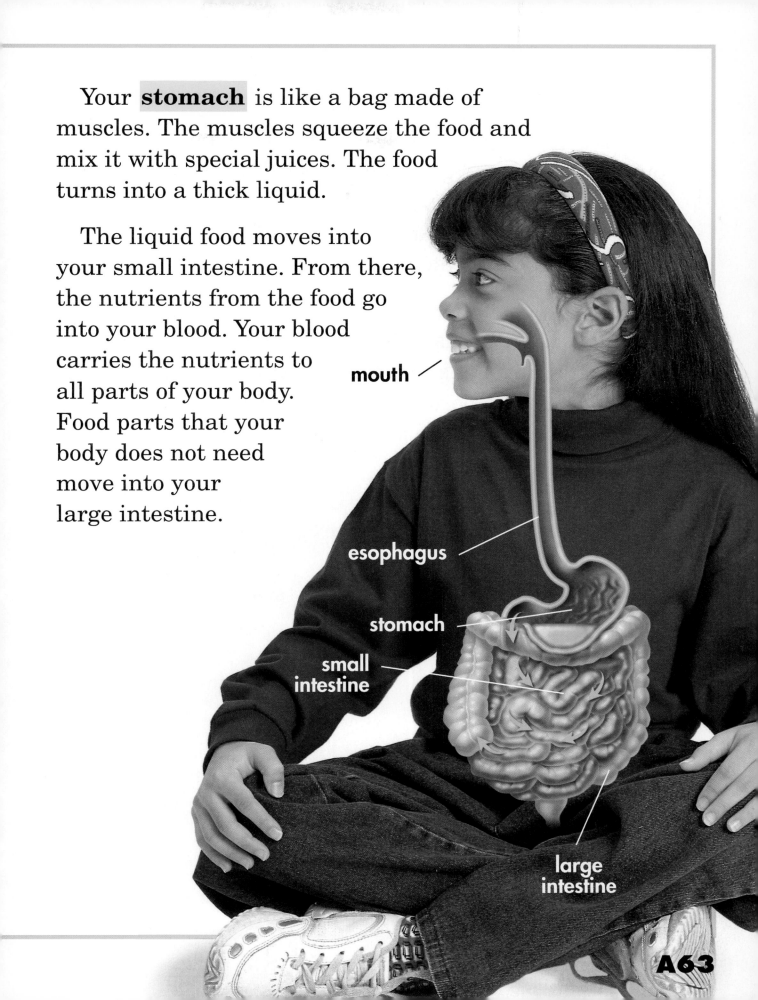

mouth

esophagus

stomach

small intestine

large intestine

Eating Healthful Foods

Healthful foods keep you healthy. They help your body grow and give you energy. Eating just one kind of food will not give your body everything it needs. You should eat different kinds of foods every day.

The Food Guide Pyramid can help you choose healthful foods. You need foods from each group. The foods you should eat the most of are at the bottom. The foods you should eat the least of are at the top.

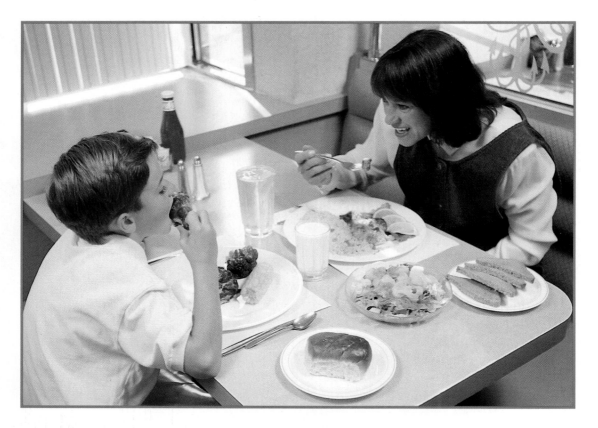

■ **What healthful foods are the boy and his mother eating?**

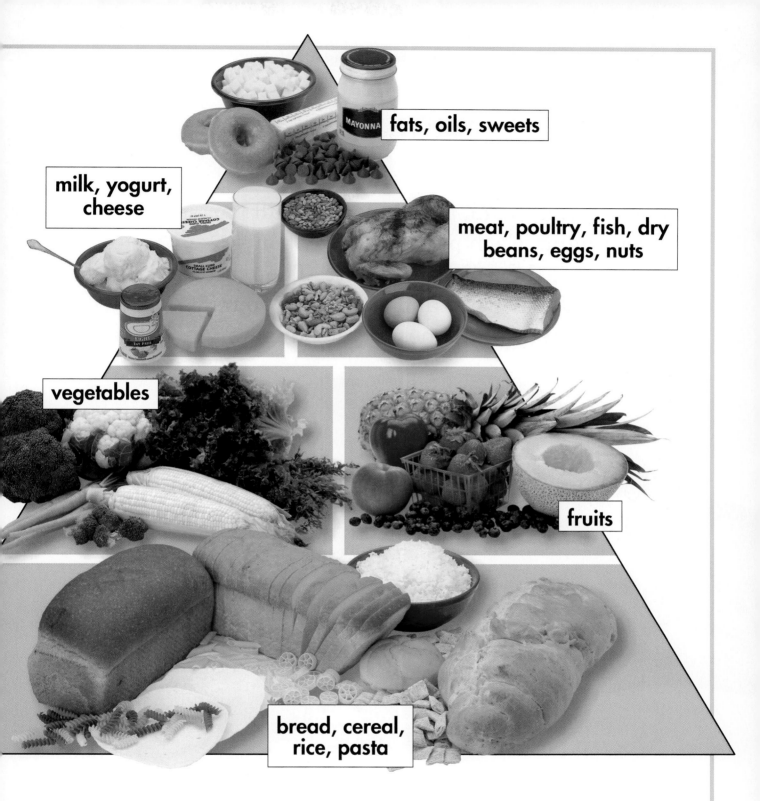

fats, oils, sweets

milk, yogurt, cheese

meat, poultry, fish, dry beans, eggs, nuts

vegetables

fruits

bread, cereal, rice, pasta

Think About It

1. How does your body digest food?
2. What are some healthful foods?

Math Link

How Many Hand Bones?

Your wrist, palm, and fingers are all parts of your hand. Each part has many bones. You can see them in this picture. There are 8 bones in your wrist and 5 bones in your palm. There are 14 bones in your fingers.

hand X ray

Think and Do

Trace your hand. Then draw in the bones. Write an addition problem to show how many bones there are in all.

A School Nurse Communicates with Students

School nurses and health aides help keep you healthy. This nurse is checking to see that this boy is growing well. A nurse also checks weight and height. He or she may take care of you when you are ill.

 Write

Write some questions you would like to ask a school nurse about staying healthy. Invite your school nurse or health aide to visit your class. Get answers to your questions.

REVIEW

Tell What You Know

1. Use the pictures to tell how people grow and change.

Vocabulary

Use the terms in the box to tell about each picture.

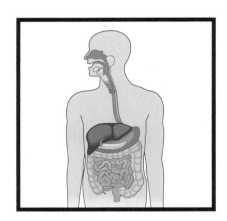

2. permanent teeth

   skeleton

   muscles

3. heart

   heart rate

   lungs

4. digest

   saliva

   esophagus

   stomach

Using Science Skills

5. Observe For two days, observe what you do to be healthy. Make a list of your observations. Then use your list to talk about how you help yourself be healthy.

6. Compare Look at a baby picture of yourself. Then make a chart like this one. How are you the same and different now?

Me		
	As a Baby	Now
Hair Color		
Eye Color		
Teeth		
Other Things		

Activities
for Home or School

Grow a Sweet Potato

1. Stick toothpicks into a sweet potato. Place the sweet potato in a jar of water.

2. Put the jar in a sunny place.

3. Observe the sweet potato for a month.

4. Draw pictures to show how the sweet potato grows and changes.

Go on an Animal Search

1. Look through magazines and books for pictures of animals.

2. List the names of the animals.

3. Group the animals. Make a chart to show your groups and tell how many of each kind you found.

4. Share your chart and list with classmates.

Animals
robins
sparrow
frog
collie
poodle

Animal Group	How Many
fish	
reptiles	
amphibians	
birds	//
mammals	

Measure Shoe Lengths

1. Trace your shoe and the shoe of an adult.

2. Measure how long each drawing is. Write the two measurements.

3. Subtract to find the difference between the two.

4. Infer what happens to children's feet over time.

Observe a Plant Without Leaves

1. Take all the leaves off a small plant.

2. Set the plant in a sunny place, and keep the plant watered.

3. Predict what will happen.

4. Observe the plant every day.

5. Draw pictures to show what happens.

The Jackson Zoo, Jackson, Mississippi

At this zoo, you can learn about animals from around the world. You can see how animals live. You can also learn about how the zoo helps animals.

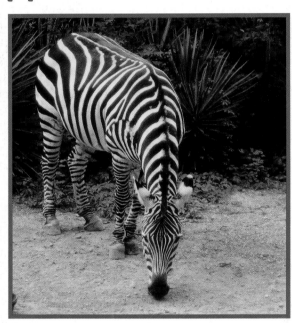

Plan Your Own Expedition

Visit a zoo or a park near you. Or log on to The Learning Site.

GO ONLINE www.harcourtschool.com

Homes for Living Things

UNIT EXPERIMENT

Plants and Pollution

As you do this unit, you will find out how pollution, or waste, hurts living things. Plan and do a test to find out how water pollution changes plants.

Habitats for Plants and Animals

Vocabulary

environment
habitat
desert
rain forest
forest
tundra
pond
adaptation
camouflage
migrate
hibernate
estivate
food chain

Did You Know?
About half of all the kinds of plants and animals on Earth live in the **rain forest**.

Scientists observe and study wolves at Wolf Park. Some wolves at the park live alone. Others live in packs. The scientists want to know how the wolves get along with one another. They also want to know other things about the way wolves live. As scientists learn more about wolves, they can better understand and help wolves.

wolf at Wolf Park

Fewer than twenty wolves live in Wolf Park. Scientists can not learn everything about wolves by observing this small group of wolves. But by observing even this small number, scientists can find out a lot about how larger numbers of wolves live in the wild.

Think About It

1. How do people learn about wolves at Wolf Park?
2. How can scientists find out about wolves by studying just a small group of them?

Social Studies Link

Roles in Communities

mother wolf with her young

Write about roles people have in their communities and families. How are these roles like roles wolves have in their packs?

Math Link

Estimating with Weights

A bison can weigh as much as 2,000 pounds. A wolf can weigh as much as 110 pounds. Estimate to find out about how many large wolves weigh as much as a large bison. Why is it often useful to estimate?

wolf and bison

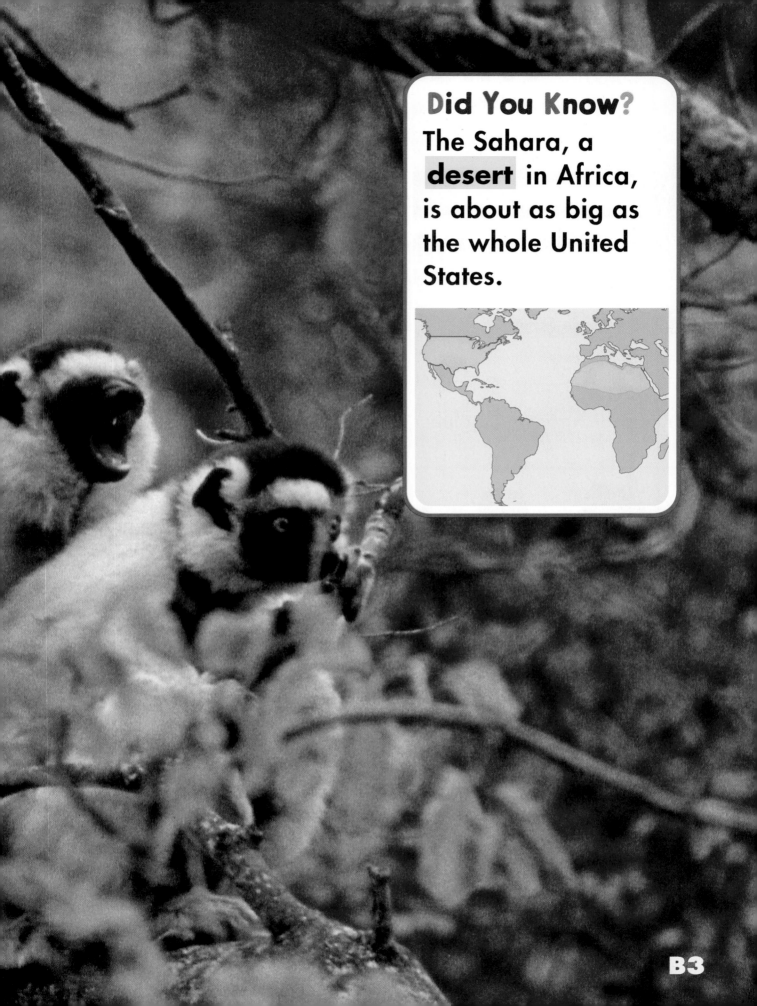

Did You Know?
The Sahara, a **desert** in Africa, is about as big as the whole United States.

B3

What Is a Habitat?

Where Animals Can Meet Their Needs

You will need

animal pictures

glue

crayons

paper and pencil

1 Choose an animal picture. Glue it in the middle of your paper.

2 On another sheet of paper, make a list of your animal's needs.

3 Draw the things your animal needs. Use your picture to communicate your ideas.

Science Skill

When you communicate your ideas, you tell or show others what you know.

Where Animals Live

Animals live in different environments around the world. An **environment** is made up of all the living and nonliving things in a place. These caribou live in a cold environment.

Alaska

Animal Habitats

Every animal has a habitat. A **habitat** is a place where an animal finds the food and water it needs to live. An animal also finds shelter there.

An environment may have many different habitats. In a forest environment, part of the forest may be the habitat of a bear. One tree in the forest may be the habitat of a wasp.

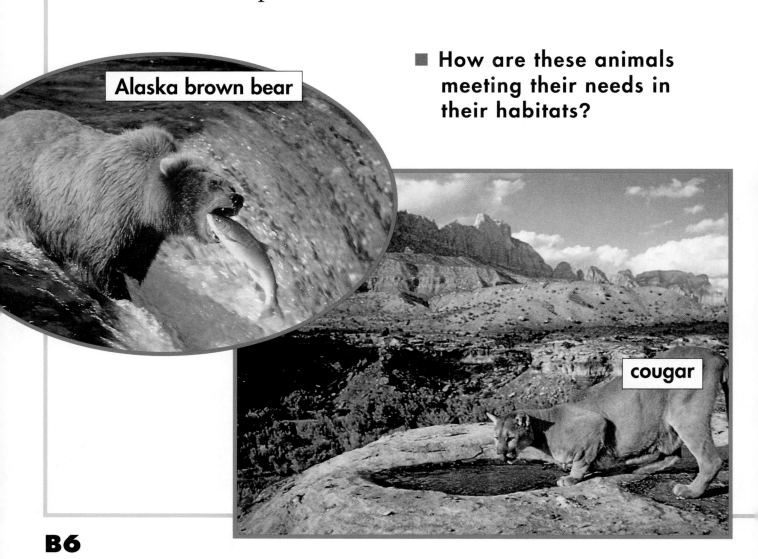

paper wasp

Alaska brown bear

■ How are these animals meeting their needs in their habitats?

cougar

grebe

Animals find habitats where they can meet their needs. A pelican eats fish, so it lives by the ocean. It can easily find fish there.

sea otter

■ **How are these animals meeting their needs in their water habitats?**

pelican

Think About It

1. What is a habitat?
2. Why do different animals have different habitats?

What Are Different Land Habitats?

Different Animal Habitats

You will need

animal picture cards

habitat picture cards

1 Classify the cards. Put the animal cards in one group and the habitat cards in another.

2 Observe the pictures carefully. Match each animal with its habitat.

3 Compare your matches with a classmate's. Tell why you made the matches you did.

Science Skill
When you classify the cards, you look for ways the pictures go together.

B8

Different Land Habitats

Some land environments have hot weather. Others have cold weather. Some get a lot of rain, and others get very little. In each environment, animals have habitats where they can find what they need.

desert

rain forest

forest

tundra

Desert Habitats

A **desert** is an environment that gets little rain. Only a few kinds of plants and animals have habitats there. Desert plants and animals do not need much water. Most desert plants store water and use it later. Many desert animals get their water from food.

■ **How are these living things meeting their needs?**

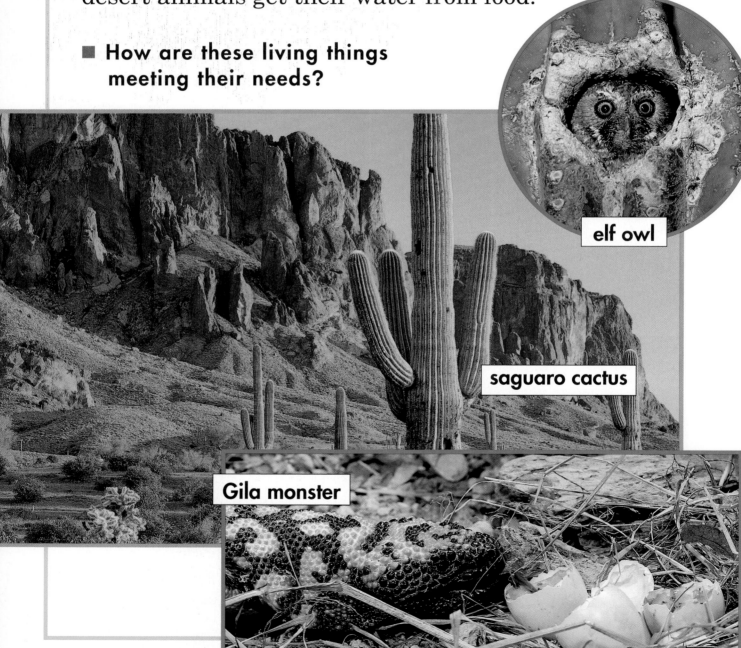

elf owl

saguaro cactus

Gila monster

Rain Forest Habitats

A **rain forest** is an environment where rain falls almost every day. Most rain forests have warm weather all year round. Many plants and animals have habitats there. The plants are used as food and shelter for the animals.

■ **How are these animals meeting their needs?**

emerald tree boa

leaf bats

tree frog

Forest Habitats

A **forest** is an environment that gets enough rain and warmth for many trees to grow. Animals in forest habitats use the trees and plants for food and shelter.

pileated woodpecker

When the weather turns cold, most of the trees in a forest lose their leaves. Some birds fly to warmer places. Some other animals sleep all winter.

■ **How are these animals meeting their needs?**

raccoons

Tundra Habitats

The **tundra** is a place with a cold, windy environment. The land is covered with ice and snow for most of the year. The summers are cool and short. A few plants can grow, but the summer is too short for trees to grow.

Only a few animals have habitats in the tundra because the winter is so cold. The polar bear's thick fur keeps it warm when it goes out to find food.

polar bear

Think About It

1. How are land environments alike? How are they different?
2. How do animals meet their needs in their land habitats?

What Are Different Water Habitats?

 Investigate

Salt Water and Fresh Water

You will need

 2 cups of water

 2 lettuce leaves

 salt and spoon

 paper and pencil

1 Mix two spoonfuls of salt into one cup of water.

2 Place a lettuce leaf in each cup of water. Leave the lettuce in the water all night.

3 Predict what will happen to each leaf. Write your predictions. Draw pictures.

4 Check the lettuce the next day. What do you observe? Did you predict correctly?

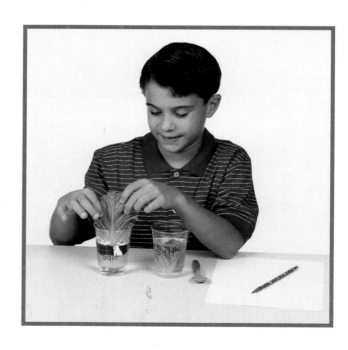

Science Skill
When you predict, you use what you know to tell what you think will happen.

Different Water Habitats

The Earth has many water environments. A **pond** is a small freshwater environment, and an ocean is a much larger saltwater environment. In each environment, plants and animals have habitats.

pond

ocean

Freshwater Habitats in a Pond

Frogs, birds, otters, and many kinds of insects live along the banks of a pond. Otters and muskrats often build burrows for shelter. Turtles, fish, and water plants live in the pond water.

muskrat

snapping turtle

The surface, or top, of the pond is the habitat of water lilies and other plants. Frogs and turtles use these plants for shelter. Some pond animals, such as insects, use these plants for food.

Some animals use the pond's surface when they look for food. Ducks and water spiders float on the surface. From there they dive to find fish and plants underwater.

■ **Why do you think this spider takes a bubble of air underwater?**

fishing spider

saltwater fish

Saltwater Habitats in the Ocean

An ocean is a large body of salt water. Plantlike algae live near the ocean's surface. Algae are food for fish and other ocean animals.

Most ocean animals swim to places where they can find food. Ocean mammals, such as whales and dolphins, must come to the surface to breathe air.

dolphins

bull's-eye lobster

Animals such as lobsters and crabs live on the ocean floor. The parts of the ocean floor that get sunlight have many plants. Some of the animals that live there eat these plants.

Think About It

1. What are some freshwater habitats?
2. What are some saltwater habitats?

A person who studies the ocean is called an oceanographer. Jacques-Yves Cousteau was a famous French oceanographer. He studied the plants and animals that live in the ocean environment.

What Are Some Animal Adaptations?

How Color Helps an Ant

You will need

paper squares

black paper

clock

1. Place the same number of red and black squares on the black paper. Form a hypothesis about which squares will be easier to see and count.

2. Count red squares for 5 seconds. Record the number. Count black squares for 5 seconds. Record the number.

3. Which squares were easier to see and count? Was your hypothesis correct? What can you infer about how color can help an ant?

Science Skill
When you form a hypothesis, you make a statement about something you can test.

Animal Adaptations

An animal's color may help protect it in its environment. An animal's body covering may also help. The ways an animal moves and behaves may help, too. An **adaptation** is anything about an animal that helps it live in its environment.

chameleon

Camouflage

One animal adaptation is camouflage. **Camouflage** is a way an animal looks that helps it hide. The color of an arctic fox's fur in winter helps it hide in its environment. Some fish have shapes that look like the tall, thin plants where they live.

arctic fox

■ **How does camouflage help these animals?**

razor fish

tiger

Some animals can hide because of patterns in their fur. A tiger's stripes help it hide in the tall grass. A zebra's stripes make it hard for other animals to pick out one zebra from the herd.

zebras

Movement and Migration

Animals move to find food or to get away from danger. The way an animal moves, such as by running or swimming, is an adaptation.

Many animals **migrate**, or travel to faraway places. Ducks and many other birds migrate to warmer places to find food in winter. Some whales and fish migrate before they have their young.

■ Why are these ducks migrating?

armadillo

Body Coverings

An animal's body covering is another adaptation. An armadillo has a covering of hard plates. The plates protect the soft parts of its body.

Differences in Animals of the Same Kind

Animals of the same kind are not all exactly alike. Some are larger or stronger. Some have thicker fur or different markings. How do these wolves look different from one another?

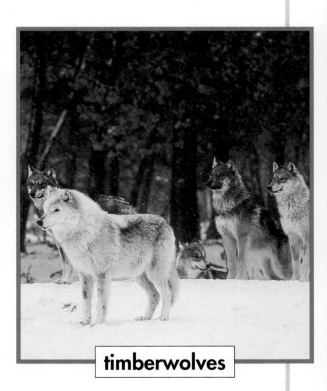
timberwolves

Other Adaptations

Some animals, such as hedgehogs, **hibernate**, or spend the winter in a deep sleep. Their body temperature falls. Their breathing slows. Their heartbeat slows, too. When they hibernate, they do not need to eat. This helps them because there is little food to find in the winter.

Some animals are not active in the winter, but they do not hibernate. Their bodies slow down, but their temperature falls only a little.

squirrel

hedgehog

black bear

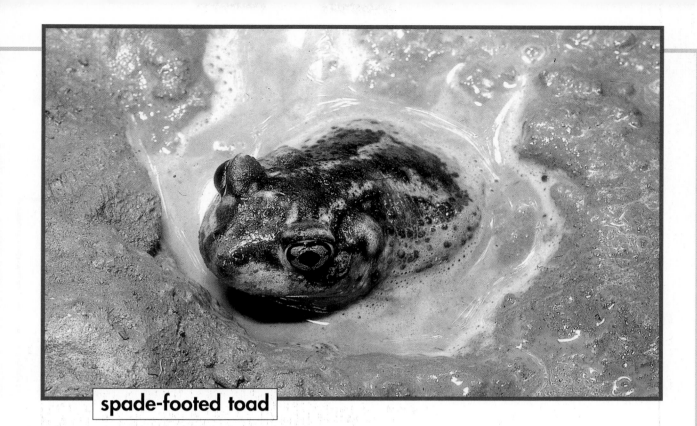

spade-footed toad

Other animals **estivate**, or stay in a deep sleep during the summer. Their bodies slow down so that they do not need food or water. This protects them from the summer's heat and dryness.

Think About It

1. What are some adaptations?
2. How are estivating and hibernating animals alike?

How Do Plants and Animals Help Each Other?

Investigate

One Way Animals Use Plants

You will need

dish of birdseed

dish of berries

paper and pencil

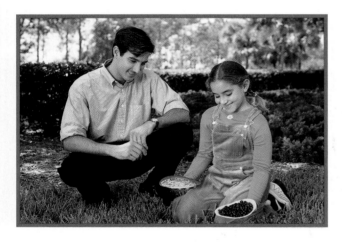

Do Birds Like Seeds or Berries?		
Like Seeds	Like Berries	Like Both

1 With your teacher, put the food outside where birds can get it.

2 Make a chart like this one. Record what you observe each day.

3 Use your chart to tell what you observed.

Science Skill

Making a chart helps you keep track of what you observe.

How Animals and Plants Help Each Other

Bees and flowers show one way animals and plants help each other. The bee helps the flower make seeds. The flower makes a sweet liquid called nectar that is food for the bee.

bumblebee

Plants Help Animals

Many animals eat plant parts. Birds eat seeds and fruits. Pandas and many other mammals eat leaves and stems.

Animals also use plants for shelter. A raccoon may live in a hole in a tree. Many birds use twigs, leaves, and grasses to build nests.

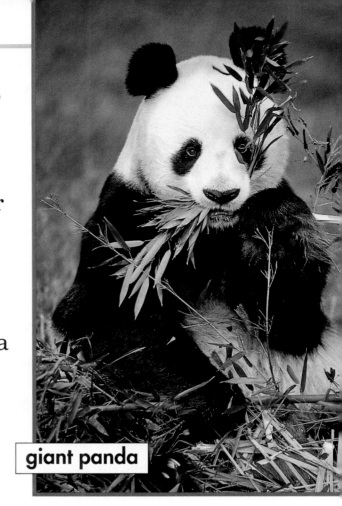

giant panda

■ **How are these animals using plants?**

American bittern

Animals Help Plants

Animals help plants by moving their seeds to new growing places. Birds eat berries that have seeds inside. Later, the seeds fall to the ground in the birds' waste. The seeds may grow into new plants far away from the plant they came from.

Seeds also stick to an animal's fur. When the animal moves, the seeds move with it. When the seeds fall off, they may land in soil and germinate.

cedar waxwing

bison

Food Chains

All living things need food to live and grow. Plants use sunlight to make their food. Some animals eat the plants. Other animals eat the plant eaters. A **food chain** is the order in which animals eat plants and other animals.

The picture shows a food chain in a pond. The food chain begins with the plants on the surface of the pond. A beetle eats the plants, and a fish eats the beetle. Then a blue heron eats the fish.

Think About It

1. How do plants and animals help each other?
2. What is a food chain?

Math Link

How Much Rain?

Rainfall and temperature make a desert and a rain forest what they are. A desert is dry. It may get less than 2 centimeters of rain in a month. A rain forest is wet. It may get more than 16 centimeters of rain in a month.

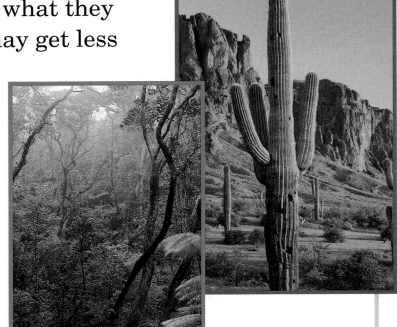

Think and Do

Measure 2 centimeters from the edge of a sheet of paper, and make a pencil mark. Make another pencil mark at 16 centimeters. How many more centimeters of rain fall in a rain forest than in a desert in a month? Show your answer as a math problem.

Byrd Baylor Observes Deserts

Byrd Baylor writes about the desert. She likes to observe the plants and animals that live there. She writes poems about the desert. One of her books of poems is called *Desert Voices*.

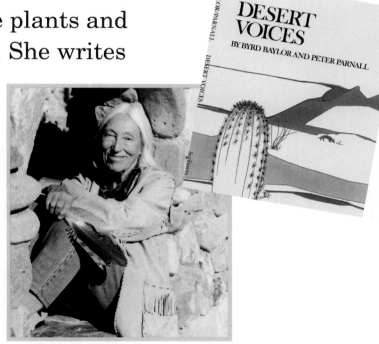

Write

Find a poem by Byrd Baylor. Share it with others. Talk about how she wrote about plants and animals. Then write your own poem about a place you enjoy.

CHAPTER 1 REVIEW

Tell What You Know

1. Tell what you know about animal adaptations. Use the words *adaptation, camouflage, migrate, hibernate,* and *estivate.*

Vocabulary

Tell which picture goes with the term.

2. tundra
3. desert
4. rain forest
5. food chain
6. pond
7. habitat

a.

b.

c.

d.

e.

f.

Using Science Skills

8. **Communicate** Draw a picture to show a food chain that includes three or more living things. Show your picture to a classmate. Talk about how the food chain works. Use the words *environment* and *food chain*.

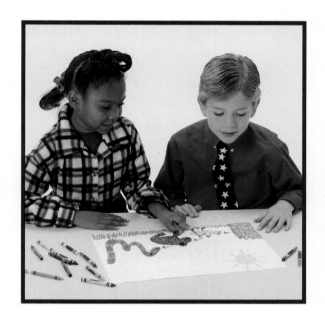

9. **Compare** Make a chart like this one to compare land environments. Then make a chart to compare water environments.

Comparing Land Environments			
Environment	Weather	Animals	Plants
desert			
rain forest			
forest			
tundra			

Changes in Habitats

Vocabulary

drought

pollution

litter

endangered

reuse

recycle

Did You Know?

If you **recycle** a stack of newspapers that is 4 feet tall, you will keep one tree from being cut down.

Did You Know?
Plants help clean up air **pollution** as they take in air.

How Does Weather Change Habitats?

Weather and Seeds

You will need

seeds

2 paper plates

4 wet paper towels

spray bottle

paper and pencil

1 Lay a wet towel on each plate. Put 4 seeds on each towel. Cover with another wet towel.

2 Put the plates in a warm place. Keep the towels on one plate wet.

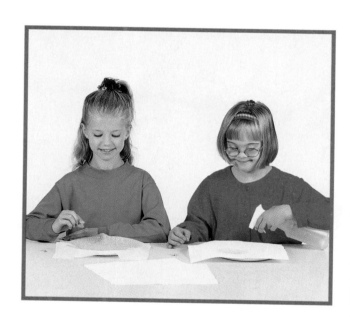

3 Check the seeds each day. Record what you observe.

4 Draw a conclusion about whether seeds outdoors need rain.

Science Skill
Use your observations and what you know to draw a conclusion.

How Rain Changes the Land

Plants and animals need certain things. Sometimes too little or too much rain changes their habitats. Then plants and animals may not have what they need.

dry wheat fields

Droughts

A pond can dry up when there is no rain for a long time. A long time without rain is called a **drought**. Without enough water, most pond plants die. Many pond animals move to other ponds.

■ How are these ponds different?

■ **How is the land in these pictures different?**

Floods

When it rains for a long time, rainwater may flood the land. Then the plants and animals get too much water. Plants die and animals move to drier places.

Lightning and Fire

Sometimes lightning strikes a tree in a forest. If the forest is dry, the tree may catch fire. The fire may burn other trees and spread through the forest.

Some animals may die. Other animals may be able to move quickly to safer places.

After a fire burns a forest, some seeds begin to germinate. Birds drop other seeds on the ground. The seeds grow into new plants, and many animals come back. Over time, the forest grows back.

■ **What conclusion can you draw from this picture?**

Think About It

1. How can too little rain or too much rain change an environment?
2. How does a fire change an environment?

How Does Pollution Change Environments?

Investigate

How Pollution Changes the Land

You will need

box   soil   objects   trowel   water

1 Put a layer of soil in the box. Place the objects on the soil.

2 Cover the objects with more soil. Place the box next to a sunny window.

3 Sprinkle water on the soil three times during the week. After one week, uncover the objects. Record what you observe. Cover the objects.

4 Repeat Step 3 each week for one month.

Science Skill
When you observe, you use your senses to learn what happens.

How Pollution Changes an Environment

Waste that harms land, water, or air is called **pollution**. Pollution also harms the plants and animals that use the land, water, and air.

Land Pollution

Trash that people do not put in a trash can is called **litter**. Litter covers up plants so light does not reach them. Animals may eat litter and get sick. If litter is caught around their bodies, animals may have trouble moving and eating.

■ **How is litter harming this bird?**

Air Pollution

Plants and animals need clean air. Air gets dirty, or polluted, when some factories and cars put out smoke and fumes. This air pollution can make plants and animals sick.

■ **What is polluting the air?**

Water Pollution

All living things need clean water. Water pollution changes rivers, lakes, and streams. Waste from factories, farms, and other places can harm plants and animals.

One animal that has been hurt by water pollution is the sea turtle. Because of pollution and other reasons, many kinds of sea turtles are **endangered**. This means that there is a danger that no more sea turtles would be alive.

Think About It

1. What are some kinds of pollution?
2. How does pollution harm plants and animals?

How Do People Help the Environment?

 Investigate

How Things Can Be Reused

You will need

used things

markers or paint

glue

newspaper

1 Observe the used things. Could you use them to make something new?

2 List the steps you plan to take. Follow your plan.

3 Use your plan to communicate to a classmate how you made something new.

Science Skill
When you list the steps you plan to take, you make it easier to communicate them.

Ways People Help the Environment

People can take care of their environment and keep it clean. They can pick up litter and make less trash. How are these people helping the environment?

Taking Care of the Land

Some people plant trees. These trees may become new homes for animals. The roots of the trees hold the soil so it will not blow away or wash away.

People take care of the land when they put litter in trash cans. In many places, people work together to pick up litter.

■ **How are these people taking care of the land?**

Making less trash is another way people can take care of the land. People decided to **reuse**, or use again, old tires to build this playground.

People also make less trash by recycling. To **recycle** means to use old materials to make new things. Metal cans and plastic bottles may be melted down to make other things.

Taking Care of the Air

People can take care of the air by making less pollution. People sometimes choose to walk or ride bicycles instead of driving their cars everywhere. Many factories have found ways to put less pollution in the air.

■ **What is this person doing to help keep the air clean?**

Taking Care of the Water

People can help keep water clean in rivers, lakes, streams, and oceans. Some people help by picking up litter. Many factory owners and farmers are finding ways to get rid of waste without putting it into the water.

■ **How are these people helping take care of the water?**

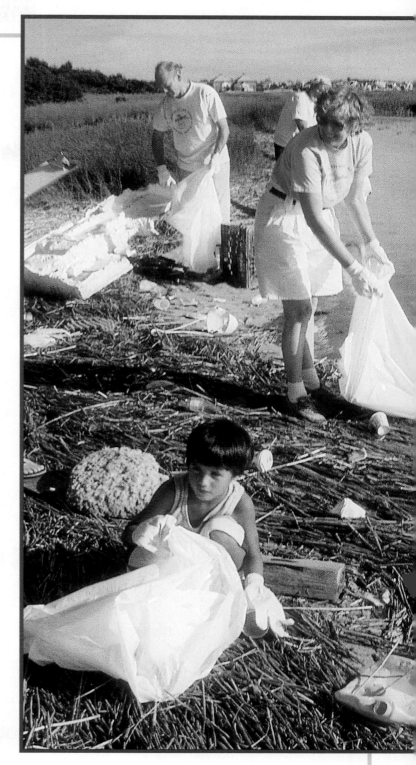

Think About It

1. How can people keep the environment clean?
2. What are some ways people can make less pollution?

Math Link

How Much Paper Trash Could You Reuse?

A landfill has many kinds of trash. It may have old bottles, empty cans, and even broken television sets. Paper is what takes up the most space in a landfill.

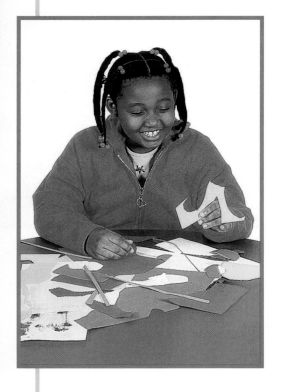

Think and Do

Keep a large bag at the front of the classroom for one day. Throw all your paper trash in it.

At the end of the day, count the papers you could reuse. Then count the papers you could not reuse. Compare. Are there more papers you could reuse or more papers you could not reuse?

Archaeologists Investigate Trash

Long ago, many people threw their trash into holes in the ground. Today archaeologists dig up the trash in these holes. Archaeologists are scientists who study how people lived long ago.

The trash helps them learn more about the people who threw it away. A broken toy may show that a family had a child. A jar may show what people liked to eat.

Write

Check your classroom trash and make a chart like this one. Write a sentence to tell what each piece of trash tells about your class.

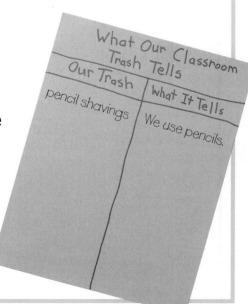

What Our Classroom Trash Tells

Our Trash	What It Tells
pencil shavings	We use pencils.

Tell What You Know

Tell what you know about each picture.

1.

2.

3.

4.

Vocabulary

Match each word with a picture that shows its meaning.

5. pollution

6. recycle

7. endangered

8. reuse

a.

b.

c.

d.

Using Science Skills

9. Draw Conclusions These two pictures show the same stream.

before   after

What conclusion can you draw about what happened to the stream?

10. Compare What things do your school and your neighborhood recycle? Make a chart like this one. Compare the things you see being recycled at school and in your neighborhood.

Things I See Recycled		
Objects	School	Neighborhood
Glass Bottles		✓
Paper	✓	✓

Activities
for Home or School

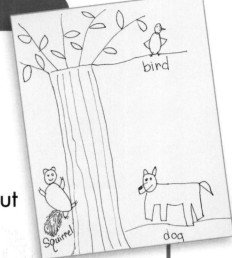

Nature Walk

1. Take a nature walk with an adult family member or your class.

2. Observe as many different animals as you can.

3. Take notes. Draw pictures and write about how these animals meet their needs.

4. Share your notes.

Make an Earthworm Habitat

1. Fill a large jar with soil. Sprinkle water on the soil.

2. Place earthworms on the soil.

3. Sprinkle soil and leaves over the earthworms.

4. Observe the habitat for several days. Draw and write to tell how the earthworms use their habitat.

5. Return the earthworms outdoors.

Recycle and Reuse

Make a recycling chart. Show the kinds of things recycled or reused.

See What Is in the Air

1. Spread petroleum jelly on the center of an index card.
2. Place the card outdoors on a windowsill.
3. The next day observe the card with a hand lens.
4. Draw and write about what you see.
5. Put another card in a different place. Do the activity again. Compare what happens.

Little River Canyon National Preserve, Fort Payne, Alabama

At this preserve, you can see how water has made a habitat for plants and animals. You can also see how plants and animals help each other.

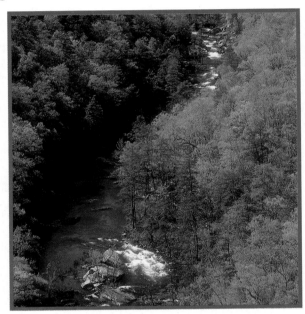

Plan Your Own Expedition

Visit a preserve or a park near you. Or log on to The Learning Site.

GO ONLINE   www.harcourtschool.com

Science in Indiana

Exploring Earth's Surface

Bluespring Caverns Park

In this unit you will learn about the Earth. At Bluespring Caverns Park in Bedford, visitors can see some of the Earth's natural resources and interesting landforms.

Bedford

The Bluespring Caverns are underground caves. Over time they were cut from limestone by flowing water. Today the caverns have more than 20 miles of underground passages. Caverns like these exist in Indiana but are rare in most of the world.

Inside the caverns, visitors can ride in a boat on the Myst'ry River. The light from this boat gives the only light in the caverns. It is very dark underground because no sunlight can get inside.

As the boat moves through the passages, visitors can see blind fish and crayfish that live in the darkness.

Think About It

1. What caused the caverns to form?
2. Why are the fish in the caverns blind?

Writing Link

Investigate Indiana Rocks and Sand

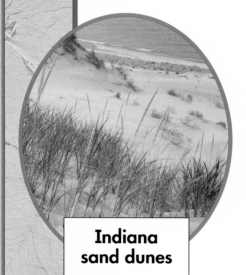

Indiana sand dunes

Investigate Earth materials found in Indiana, such as rocks and sand. Look at pictures of boulders. After you observe these Earth materials, describe them. Note their sizes, shapes, and so on. Compare your observations with those of classmates. If you disagree, what new observations can you make?

Math Link

How Much Paper?

Find out how much paper is recycled in Indiana each year. Estimate how much paper you could recycle in one day. Using that number, estimate the amount you could recycle in one week. Then recycle paper for one week. How close was your estimate to the amount you actually recycled?

paper recycling

Exploring Earth's Surface

UNIT EXPERIMENT

Plants and Erosion

As you do this unit, you will find out about the uses of plants. Plan and do a test to find out how plants keep soil from being washed away.

Earth's Resources

Vocabulary

rock

soil

resource

natural resource

medicine

transportation

Did You Know?

In Hawaii, the black sand on some beaches is made up of pieces of **rock** from a nearby volcano.

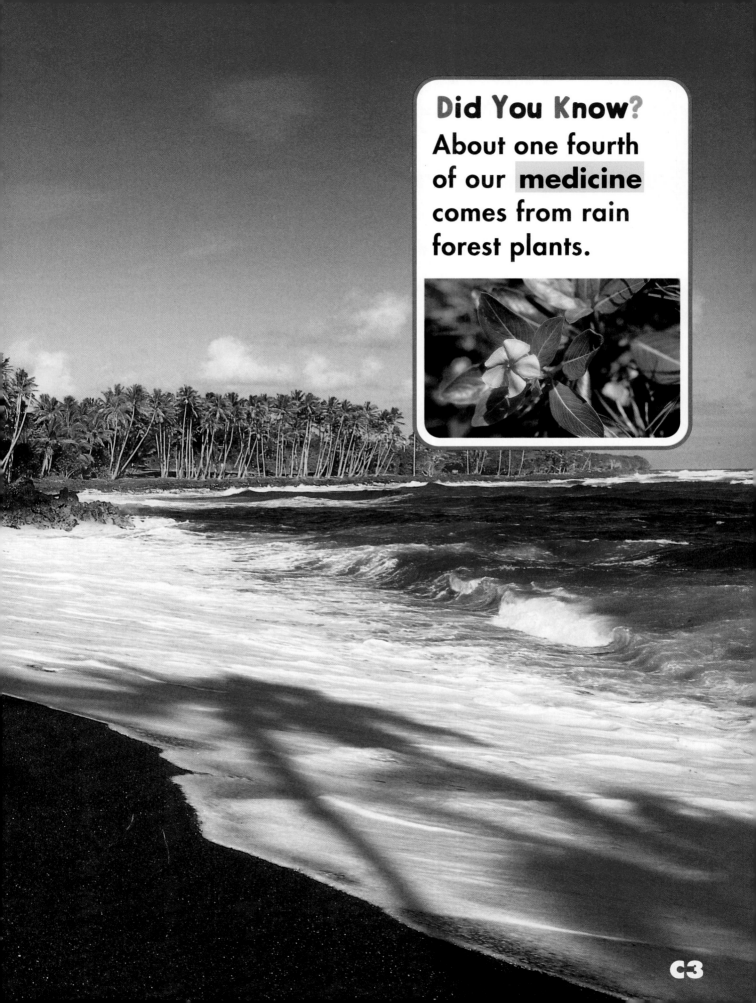

Did You Know?
About one fourth of our **medicine** comes from rain forest plants.

How Do People Use Rocks and Soil?

A Way to Use Soil

You will need

clay

ice cube tray

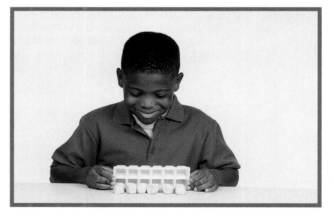

1 Make some clay bricks. Fill an ice cube tray with clay.

2 Put the tray in a warm, sunny place. Take the bricks out when they are hard.

3 What happened to the bricks? Infer why you put the bricks in the sun.

Science Skill

When you infer information, you can figure out why something happened.

Ways That People Use Rocks and Soil

A **rock** is a hard, nonliving thing that comes from the Earth. The loose top layer of the Earth's surface is **soil**. People use rocks and soil in different ways.

Ways That People Use Rocks

Rocks are a kind of natural resource. A **resource** is anything that people can use. A **natural resource** is something found in nature that people can use to meet their needs.

boulder

People use rocks to build things, such as houses and roads. They also use rocks to make sculptures.

People may change the size, shape, and texture, or feel, of rocks. They break big rocks into smaller rocks to make gravel for roads. They make parts of sculptures rough and smooth.

Mount Rushmore

truck dumping gravel

■ How are the rocks in the truck being used?

Ways That People Use Soil

People use soil to grow food and to make bricks. One kind of brick is called adobe. People make a mix of wet clay and straw and shape it into bricks. They use the hard bricks to build things.

potato field

adobe building

Think About It

1. How do people use rocks?
2. How do people use soil?

How Do People Use Plants?

 Investigate

Using Plants to Make a Bird Feeder

You will need

milk carton   scissors   plant parts   glue   birdseed

1 With your teacher, cut the top off a milk carton.

CAUTION Cut carefully.

2 Glue plant parts to the sides and bottom of the carton.

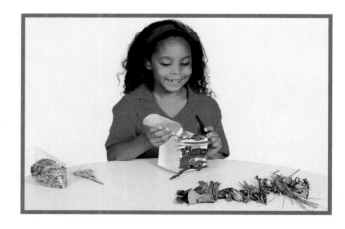

3 Put birdseed in your feeder, and place it outside.

4 Communicate to classmates what you did.

Science Skill
You can show things to communicate about them.

Ways That People Use Plants

Plants are another important natural resource. They have many uses. People enjoy looking at plants. They use them to make the surroundings more beautiful.

plants at Callaway Gardens, Georgia

Furniture and Paper

Plants are a resource that people use to make many products. People use wood from trees to build furniture and houses.

People also use wood to make paper. They make wood chips into a wet, woody mix called pulp. Then they press the pulp flat to make sheets of paper.

■ **How have people used plants here?**

pine tree

pine stool

newspapers

Cloth and Fuel

People also make cloth from plants. They use the cotton plant to make cloth for clothes, sheets, and many other products.

People also burn plants for fuel. They may use branches that have fallen from a tree to make a campfire. They may make fireplace logs from newspaper.

cotton boll

cotton hat

■ **How are plants being used here?**

Food, Oils, and Spices

People use plants for food. They eat fruits and vegetables. They use other plant parts to make foods such as bread and pasta. They also use plant parts to make cooking oils and spices, which flavor foods.

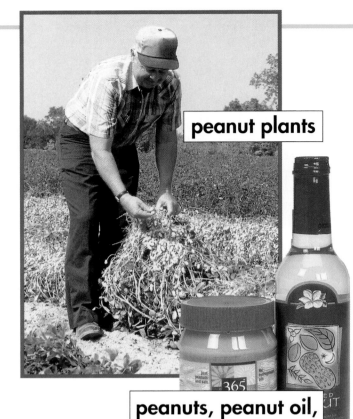

peanut plants

peanuts, peanut oil, and peanut butter

■ **How is this girl using plants?**

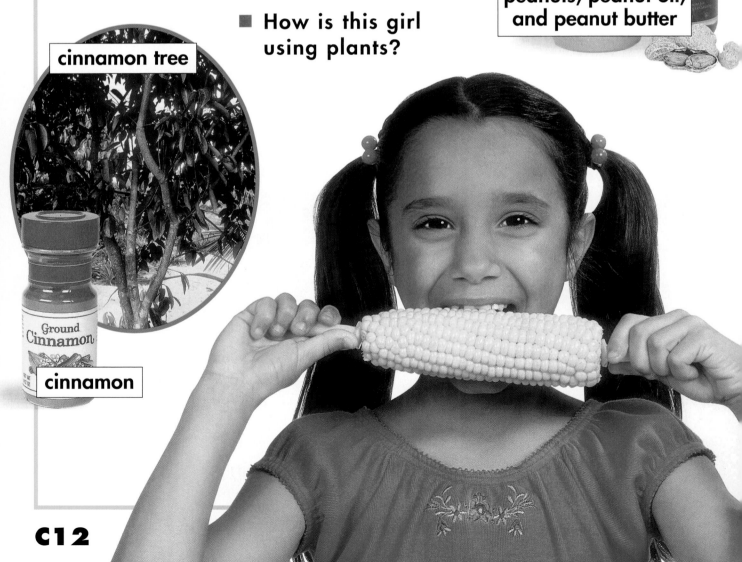

cinnamon tree

Ground Cinnamon

cinnamon

Medicine and Rubber

Plants are also used to make many medicines. A **medicine** is a product that helps people who are ill or in pain.

Many plants have a liquid called latex. The latex from some plants is used to make rubber. Then the rubber is used to make products such as car and bicycle tires.

aloe plant and aloe product

rubber bicycle tires

rubber tree

Think About It

1. How do people use plants for food?
2. What are some other ways people use plants?

How Do People Use Water?

Investigate

How You Use Water

How Our Class Uses Water in One Day	
How Our Class Uses Water	How Many Times
drinking	
washing hands	
watering plants	
cleaning	

1 Keep track of the ways your class uses water in one day. Collect the data in a chart.

2 Make a tally mark each time your class uses water. After a day, count the marks.

3 Use your data to answer these questions.
- How many ways did your class use water?
- Which way did your class use water most?

Science Skill
Collecting data is one way to find the answers to your questions.

Ways That People Use Water

Water is a natural resource that people use every day. People drink water, but they also use it for swimming, transportation, and cleaning. How are people using water here?

Uses for Water

People, plants, and animals need water to live and grow. People use water for drinking, cooking, bathing, and watering plants. They also use it for washing clothes, dishes, and cars.

■ How are these children using water?

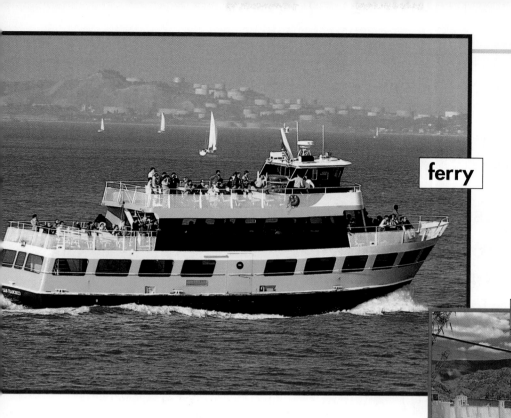

ferry

Hoover Dam

People also use water when they sail boats and ships. Boats and ships are kinds of **transportation**, or ways to move people or things.

Water is also used to make electricity. People build dams on rivers. The flow of the river turns machines that make electricity.

Think About It

1. How do people use water to care for plants and animals?
2. What are some other ways people use water?

Math Link

How Much Water?

Most people use about 100 gallons of water each day. They use the water for drinking, keeping clean, and cooking. They also use it for washing clothes, dishes, and pets.

Write

It takes about 2 gallons of water to wash your hands and face. If 4 people in a family wash their hands and faces, how much water will they use? Write an addition story to show the answer.

There are 4 people in a family. They

An Artist Uses Natural Resources

Maya Lin is an architect and artist who works with stone and other natural materials. She has designed sculptures made of granite and has even used water in her work. Lin designed an earth sculpture called "The Wave Field." It is made of soil covered with grass.

Think and Do

Design your own sculpture. First draw a picture of what your sculpture will look like. Use rocks, soil, and plant parts to make your sculpture.

Tell What You Know

1. How does the picture show ways people use natural resources?

Vocabulary

Tell which picture goes with each word.

2. rock

3. medicine

4. soil

5. transportation

a.

b.

c.

d.

Using Science Skills

6. Make Models/Communicate

Make a model boat to show one way people use water. Decide what you will use to make your model. You could use clay, paper, or an empty milk carton.

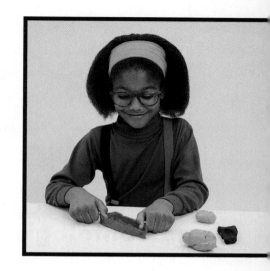

Write one sentence that tells how your model boat uses water. Write another sentence that tells what resources you used to make it.

7. Collect Data/Communicate

Make a chart to show ways people use three resources. Draw or cut out pictures that show some ways that each resource is used. Glue your pictures in the chart. Then share your chart.

How People Use Resources		
Soil	Plants	Water

Earth Long Ago

Vocabulary

fossil

paleontologist

reconstruct

extinct

dinosaur

Triceratops

Did You Know?
Plant-eating **dinosaurs** were the largest land animals that ever lived on Earth.

Did You Know?
The moa was a bird 10 feet tall that became **extinct** about 300 years ago.

What Is a Fossil?

How Some Fossils Get Their Shapes

You will need

clay

small objects

1 Break the clay into four pieces. Press each piece flat.

2 Press a different object into each piece to make a print. Remove the object.

3 Have classmates infer which object made each print.

Science Skill
You can use clues to infer information.

Fossils

Plants and animals lived on the Earth before people did. People know this because they have found fossils. A **fossil** is what is left of a plant or an animal that lived long ago.

fossil

How Fossils Are Made

Some plants and animals that died millions of years ago were eaten. Many rotted away. Other plants and animals became fossils.

fish fossil

These pictures show one way fossils are made. A fish in the ocean dies. Its body sinks to the ocean floor. Soon the fish is covered up with mud.

■ **What is happening to the fish's body?**

How a Fossil Is Made

1 A fish dies.

2 Mud and sand cover the fish.

A **paleontologist** is a scientist who finds and studies fossils. By studying fossils, a paleontologist learns about plants and animals that lived long ago.

More mud and sand cover the fish's body as it rots away. They press on the mud for a long time until this mud turns to rock. A print of the fish is left in the rock. Prints like this are one kind of fossil.

3 The mud and sand turn to rock.

■ **What is this paleontologist doing?**

Where Fossils Are Found

Scientists find many kinds of fossils in rocks. Some are animal teeth, shells, and bones that have turned to stone. Others are plant and animal prints.

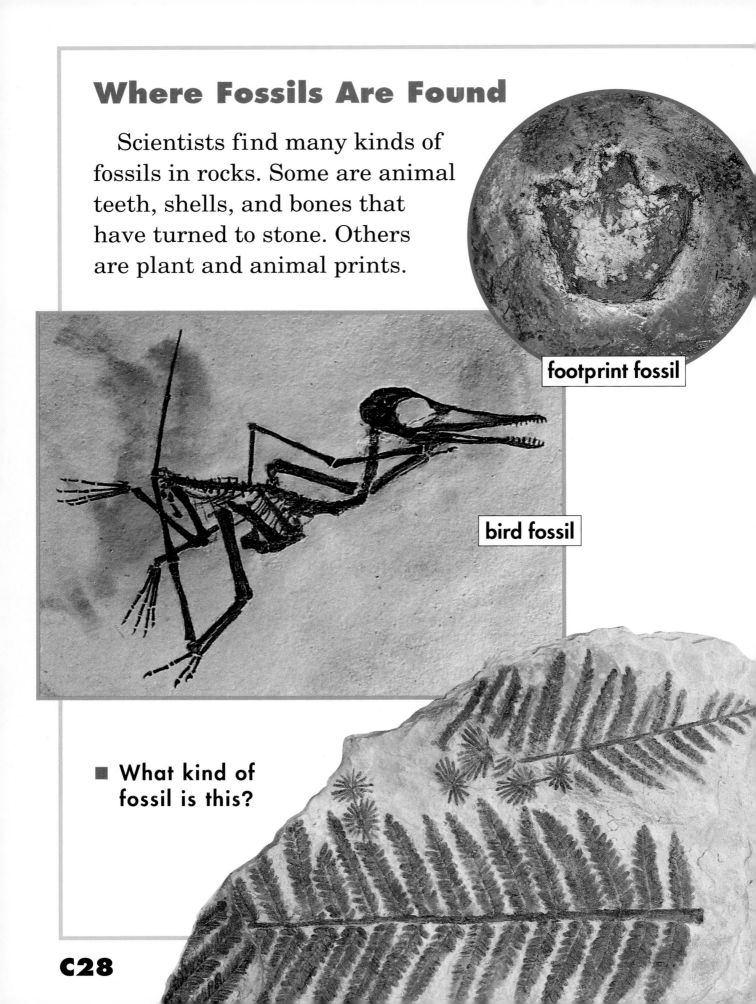

footprint fossil

bird fossil

■ What kind of fossil is this?

Scientists also find fossils in other things, such as tar and amber. Amber is the hard sap of pine trees that grew long ago.

fly in amber

saber-toothed cat fossil

mammoth fossil

Think About It

1. How are some fossils made?
2. Where are some fossils found?

What Have Scientists Learned from Fossils?

Investigate

How Scientists Find Fossils

You will need

play dough

small objects

tools

1 Hide an object in some play dough. Let the dough get hard. Trade with a classmate.

2 Use tools to find the object. Do not harm the object.

3 Communicate what you did.

Science Skill
One way to communicate is to talk with your partner about what you did.

How Scientists Get Fossils

Paleontologists find some fossils inside rocks. To get the fossils out, they must chip the rock away. They work slowly and carefully so that they do not break the fossils.

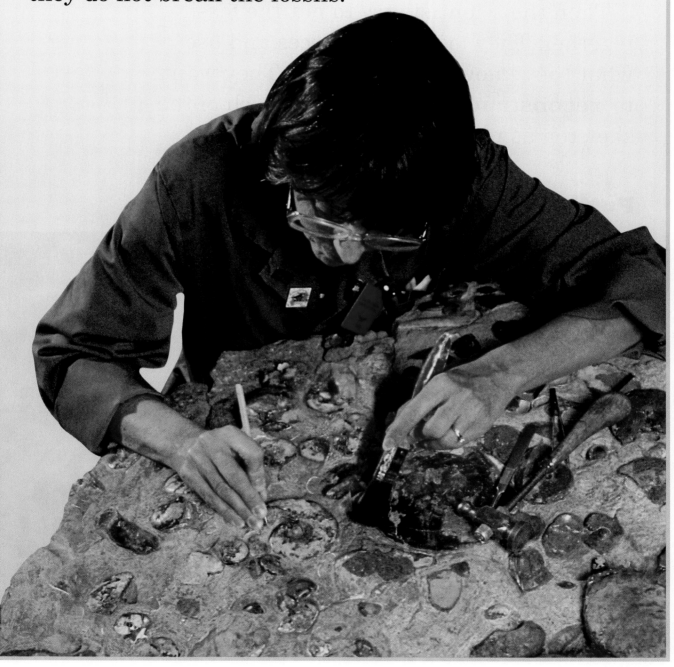

How Scientists Put Fossils Together

When scientists chip a fossil from a rock, it may be in pieces. They take the fossil pieces to a museum, where they first clean them.

Then the scientists try to put the fossil together. They look at the pieces and use what they know about animals. They want to **reconstruct**, or rebuild, as much of the skeleton as possible.

Putting Fossils Together

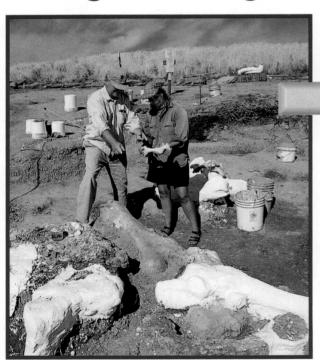

1 The fossil is taken out of the rock.

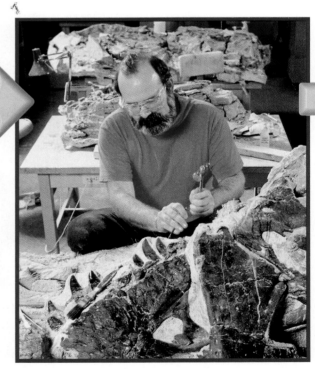

2 The pieces are cleaned.

What Scientists Learn from Fossils

Fossils help paleontologists learn about plants and animals that lived long ago. Scientists also learn from fossils how plants and animals have changed. They compare the fossils with plants and animals that live today.

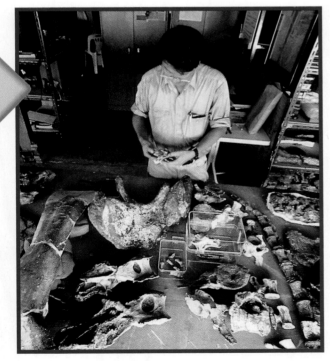

3 The fossil pieces are put together.

■ **Observe the fossil above. How do you think the living animal looked?**

C33

Comparing Animals of Long Ago and Today

Kinds of animals that are no longer living are **extinct**. Paleontologists can infer information about extinct animals. They do this by comparing them to animals that live today.

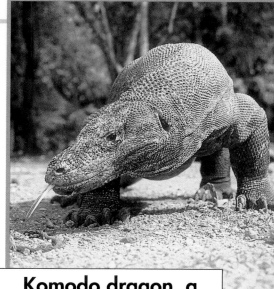

Komodo dragon, a reptile that lives today

■ **What can scientists infer about the extinct reptile?**

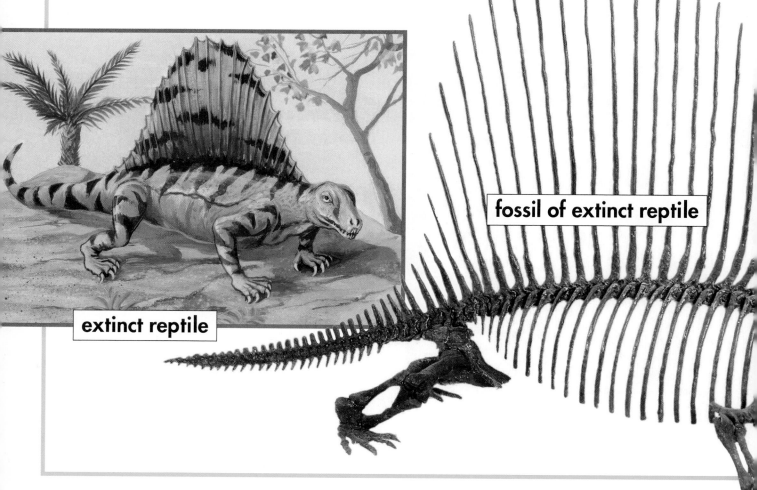

extinct reptile

fossil of extinct reptile

The anhinga is a bird with a long neck and a long, pointed bill. It lives near water and dives for fish. The extinct bird also had a long neck and a long, pointed bill. Paleontologists infer from its skeleton that the extinct bird dived for fish, too. They also infer that this bird could not fly as well as the anhinga can.

anhinga, a bird that lives today

extinct bird

fossil of extinct bird

Think About It

1. How do scientists get fossils?
2. What do scientists learn from fossils?

What Have Scientists Learned About Dinosaurs?

Investigate

Dinosaur Skeletons

You will need

scissors

books about dinosaurs

chenille sticks

1 Choose a dinosaur to make a model skeleton.

2 Twist two chenille sticks together. Shape them to make the backbone and the head.

3 Twist sticks around the backbone for legs. Cut and twist on more sticks for ribs.

 CAUTION Cut carefully.

Science Skill
Sharing your model can help you explain your ideas.

What Scientists Know About Dinosaurs

A **dinosaur** is a kind of animal that lived millions of years ago. Today dinosaurs are extinct. Paleontologists know about dinosaurs from their fossils.

dinosaur fossil

Kinds of Dinosaurs

Many kinds of dinosaurs used to live on the Earth. Some were as small as a chicken. Others were taller than a three-story building.

The word *dinosaur* means "terrible lizard." Paleontologists give each dinosaur a name that describes it. One kind of dinosaur is named **Triceratops**, which means "three-horned face."

Another dinosaur is named Tyrannosaurus rex. Its name means "tyrant lizard king." A tyrant is a harsh ruler. Tyrannosaurus rex was a large, meat-eating dinosaur.

How Tall Were Dinosaurs?

Height in Feet

24
20
16
12
8
4
0

Stegosaurus   **Triceratops**

■ **How tall was Tyrannosaurus rex?**

Tyrannosaurus rex   Diplodocus   child, age 7

What Scientists Learn About Dinosaurs

One way paleontologists learn about dinosaurs is by comparing them to animals that live today. Triceratops had flat teeth like those of today's plant-eating animals. Tyrannosaurus rex had long, pointed teeth like those of today's meat eaters.

Tyrannosaurus rex tooth

■ Compare the dinosaur teeth. How are they different?

Triceratops tooth

Scientists have found fossil prints of dinosaur skin. These fossils show that some dinosaurs had scaly skin. Others had smoother skin.

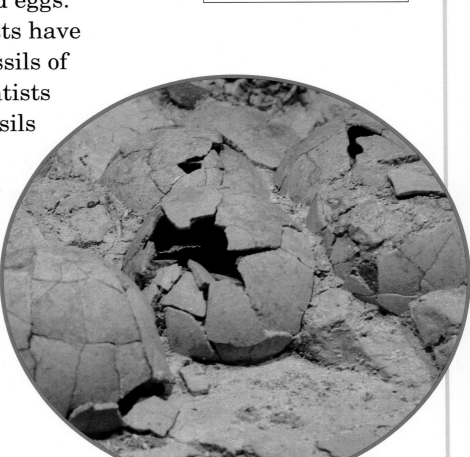

dinosaur skin fossil

Scientists know that some dinosaurs laid eggs. Fossil dinosaur nests have been found with fossils of eggs in them. Scientists have also found fossils of young dinosaurs around some nests.

■ **What is in this dinosaur nest?**

Think About It

1. How do scientists learn about dinosaurs?

2. What have scientists found out about dinosaurs?

Math Link

Compare Dinosaur Sizes

Scientists know from fossils that dinosaurs were many sizes. Compsognathus was about 2 feet long. Scelidosaurus was about 12 feet long. Stegosaurus was larger. It was about 20 feet long.

Compsognathus

Scelidosaurus

Stegosaurus

Write

Make a bar graph to compare the lengths of these dinosaurs. Then use your graph to write about which dinosaur was the longest and which was the shortest.

Dinosaur Lengths in Feet										
Compsognathus										
Scelidosaurus										
Stegosaurus										

0 2 4 6 8 10 12 14 16 18 20

No More Brontosaurus

Paleontologists found fossils of a kind of dinosaur they named Apatosaurus. Then they found bone fossils that looked the same but were bigger. They thought they had found a different kind of dinosaur and called it Brontosaurus.

Later, scientists figured out that both sets of fossils were from Apatosaurus bones. The name Brontosaurus is not used anymore.

Think and Do

Find out what it might be like to fit fossils together. Draw two pictures of the same kind of animal, but make one larger. Cut out each body part. Mix up the body parts of both animals. Trade with a classmate. Try to put each of your classmate's two pictures together.

Tell What You Know

1. Tell what you know about each picture.

Vocabulary

Use these words to tell about the picture.

2. fossil

3. dinosaur

4. extinct

5. Triceratops

6. paleontologist

7. reconstruct

Using Science Skills

8. **Make a Model** This is a trilobite fossil. A trilobite was an animal that lived in the ocean millions of years ago. It was about 8 to 10 centimeters, or 3 to 4 inches, long.

   Use clay and a pencil tip to make a model of a trilobite fossil. Use your model to tell a classmate about trilobites.

9. **Infer** The table shows the teeth of two dinosaurs. Copy the table. Write what each dinosaur ate and how you know.

Dinosaur Teeth and What Dinosaurs Ate			
Dinosaur	Shape of Tooth	What It Ate	How I Know
Tyrannosaurus			
Triceratops			

Activities
for Home or School

Make Watercolor Pictures

1. Paint a picture with watercolor paint. Let the painting dry.

2. Observe the paper. What has happened to the water in the paint? How can you tell?

3. Write about what you observe.

Soil Nutrients Study

1. With an adult, collect once-living things such as a berry, a stick, and a leaf.

2. Bury each object outside in its own hole about 4 inches deep.

3. Mark each spot. Check the objects once a week for four weeks.

4. Record what you observe.

5. Draw a conclusion.

Water in Soil

1. Place some soil on a paper towel.

2. Let it stand for half an hour.

3. Shake off the soil. What is left on the towel?

4. Communicate your findings to classmates.

Make a Rock Collection

1. Collect some small rocks.

2. Observe the rocks and decide how you want to classify them.

3. Glue the rocks in groups on pieces of cardboard. Label each group.

4. Share your rock collection.

light colored rocks

dark colored rocks

The Academy of Natural Sciences, Philadelphia, Pennsylvania

At this museum, you can learn about animals and plants that lived long ago. You can visit Dinosaur Hall and see fossils. You can also dig for fossils yourself.

Plan Your Own Expedition

Visit a science center or a museum near you. Or log on to The Learning Site.

 www.harcourtschool.com
GO ONLINE

Science in Indiana

Space and Weather

Children's Science and Technology Museum of Terre Haute

Terre Haute

In this unit you will learn about space and weather. Visitors to the Children's Science and Technology Museum of Terre Haute can learn about space and many other things.

The museum lets people interact with the exhibits. One exhibit is a Space Simulator, where visitors can see what it would be like to fly a space vehicle. The museum also has other activities that teach visitors about space.

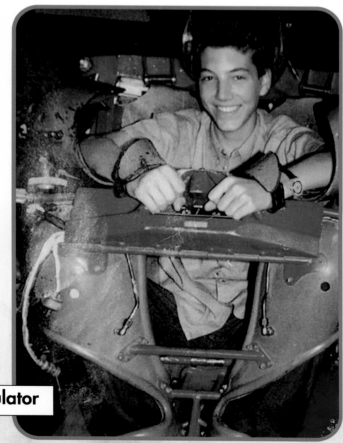

Space Simulator

Another exhibit has a pretend television studio. Visitors can see what it would be like to be on a television news show. They can act like a reporter or a weather forecaster on television.

Professor Energy

model television studio

Visitors to the museum like to see Professor Energy and Maggie. Professor Energy and Maggie are robots. These machines ride tricycles and talk with visitors to the museum.

Think About It

1. What kinds of exhibits does the museum have?
2. Think about being a weather forecaster on television. What kinds of things would you talk about?

Writing Link

Robots

The robots at the museum are machines that look like small people and can talk and ride tricycles. Of course, they are not really people. Write about ways robots and people are the same and ways they are different.

Professor Energy and visitors

Math Link

Seasonal Temperature

thermometer

Air temperature in Indiana changes from season to season. With your class, use a thermometer to measure and record the air temperature outside. Do this at the same time of day once a week for the rest of the school year. Make a graph to show temperature changes from season to season.

UNIT D EARTH SCIENCE

Space and Weather

UNIT EXPERIMENT

Puddle Shape and Evaporation

As you do this unit, you will find out how water goes into the air. Plan and do a test to find out how the shape of a puddle changes how water goes into the air.

The Solar System

Vocabulary

star

constellation

sun

planet

solar system

energy

solar energy

rotation

orbit

season

moon

moonlight

crater

Did You Know?

The **sun** is so large that more than a million Earths could fit inside it.

Did You Know?

The **moon** has no air, and the sky is always black.

What Are Stars and Planets?

Investigate

Star Pictures

You will need

"star" cups   flashlight   black paper   tape

1 Tape the paper to a wall, and choose a star cup.

2 Point the bottom of the cup toward the paper.

3 Shine the flashlight through the cup. What do you see? Record.

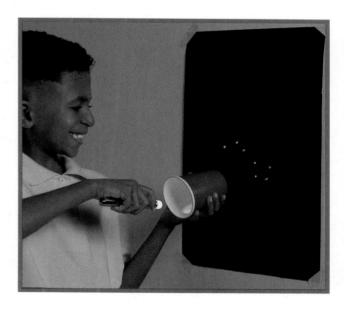

4 Repeat with the other cups. Communicate to classmates what you observe.

Science Skill

When you communicate, you tell others what you think through writing, drawing, or speaking.

The Night Sky

On a clear night, you can see many stars. There are too many of them to count. They look like small points of light in the night sky. Stars are really much bigger than Earth. They look small because they are far away.

Stars

A **star** is a big ball of hot gases. The hot gases give off light. This light is what we see from Earth. Stars may appear to twinkle.

Some stars seem brighter than others. They may look brighter because they are bigger or hotter. They may also look brighter because they are closer to Earth.

Andromeda

Milky Way

■ **Why can't you count the number of stars in the Milky Way?**

Some people use telescopes to look at the night sky. A telescope makes stars look closer and larger.

Constellations

A group of stars that form a star picture is called a **constellation**. Long ago, people saw pictures in groups of stars. They named the different star pictures.

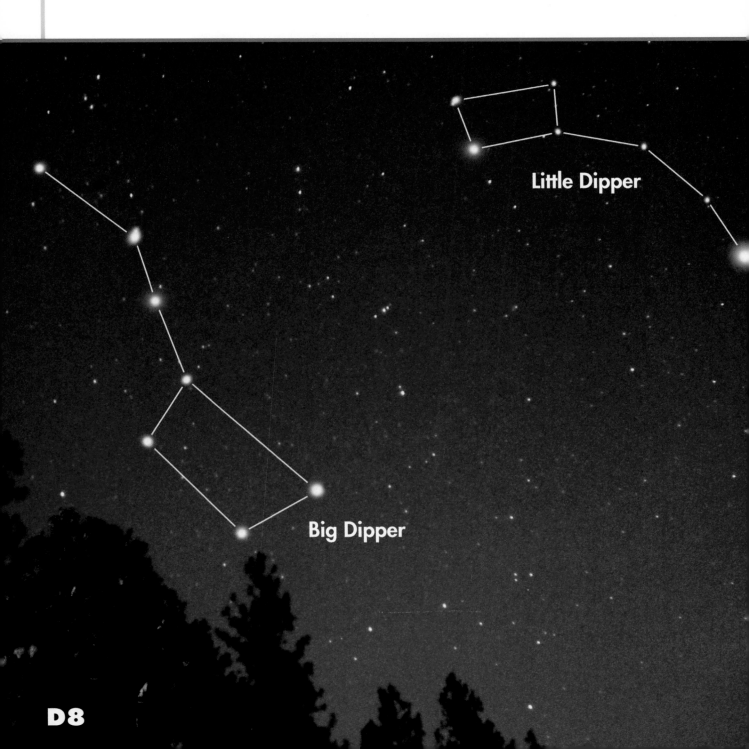

Little Dipper

Big Dipper

The entire sky has about 88 constellations. One constellation is called the Big Bear. It contains a group of seven stars called the Big Dipper. Together, these stars form the shape of a dipper, a kind of big spoon.

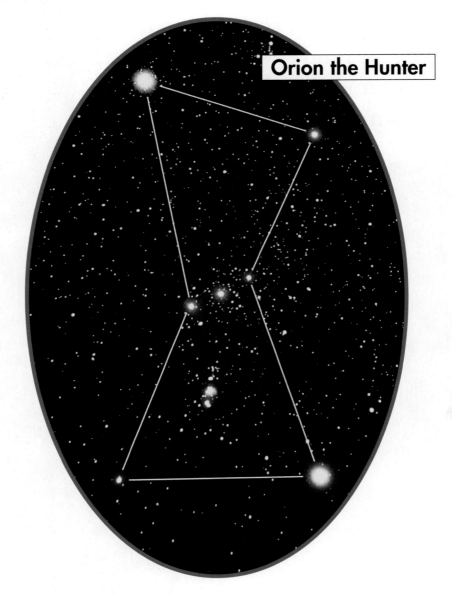

Orion the Hunter

■ **What do the star pictures on the left look like?**

The Solar System

The **sun** is the star closest to Earth. Nine planets, including Earth, move around it. A **planet** is a large ball of rock or gas that travels around the sun. Together, the sun and the planets make up our **solar system**.

■ Which planets are closest to Earth?

Mars

Earth

Venus

Mercury

sun

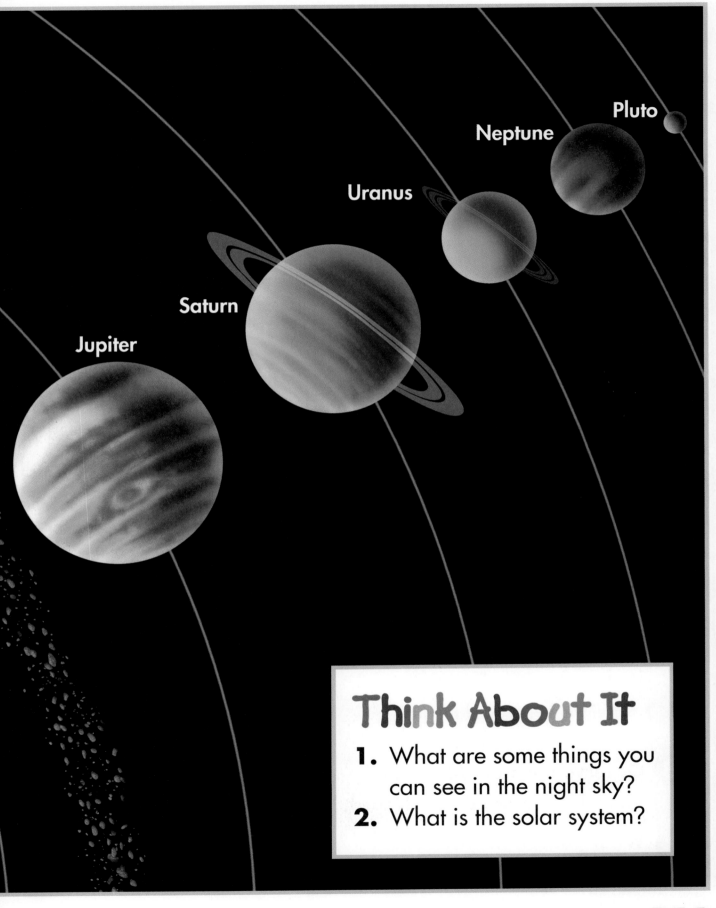

Pluto

Neptune

Uranus

Saturn

Jupiter

Think About It

1. What are some things you can see in the night sky?
2. What is the solar system?

What Causes Day and Night?

 Investigate

Where the Sun Is

You will need

paper and pencil

Where the Sun Is			
	Day 1	Day 2	Day 3
10:00 a.m.			
2:00 p.m.			

1 Observe where the sun is in the morning. Record.

CAUTION Never look directly at the sun.

2 Observe the sun from the same place in the afternoon. Record where it is now.

3 Observe the sun at the same times for 2 more days. Record.

4 What pattern do you see?

Science Skill
A pattern of something happening over and over at the same place and time is a time/space relationship.

Day and Night

Each day, the sun seems to move slowly across the sky from east to west. The sun does not really cross our sky. It is Earth that is moving. Because Earth moves, we have day and night.

sunrise

noon

sunset

The Sun

The sun is the star closest to Earth, but it is still very far away. This makes the sun look small even though it is much larger than Earth.

Like other stars, the sun is made of hot gases. The gases are so hot they give off light and heat. Light and heat are kinds of **energy** because they can cause change and do work.

sun

Most living things on Earth use **solar energy**, or light and heat from the sun. Plants use the sun's light to make food. Animals and people use its light to see in the daytime. The sun's heat warms water, land, air, and all living things on Earth.

■ **What does the sun look like here?**

Earth's Rotation

Earth is shaped something like a sphere, or a ball. It spins round and round in space. The spinning of Earth is called its **rotation**. It takes about 24 hours for Earth to rotate, or spin, all the way around one time. One full rotation of Earth is one full day.

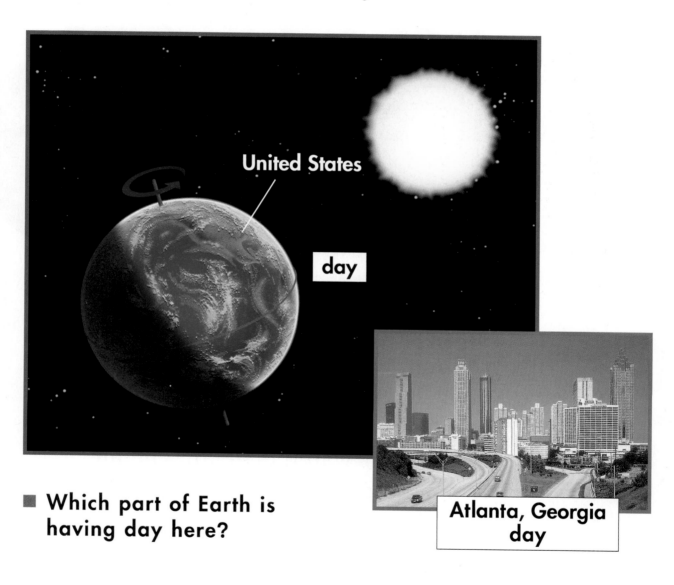

United States

day

Atlanta, Georgia
day

■ **Which part of Earth is having day here?**

The sun shines all the time, but not always on your part of Earth. Earth's rotation causes each part of Earth to have light and dark each day.

When one side of Earth faces the sun, that side is lighted, and it is daytime. The other side of Earth is dark, and it is nighttime.

United States

night

Atlanta, Georgia
night

Think About It

1. What is the sun?
2. Why does Earth have day and night?

What Causes the Seasons?

How Sunlight Shines on Earth

You will need

ball with
pencil

lamp

1 Tilt the ball so the top of the pencil points toward the light.

2 Does the light shine more brightly on the top or the bottom of the ball? Record.

3 Move the ball to the other side of the light. Keep the tilt of the pencil the same.

4 Observe where the light is brightest now. Record and discuss.

Science Skill
To observe light here, you need only your sense of sight.

What Causes the Seasons

Earth rotates on an imaginary line called an axis. Earth tilts on this axis. At the same time, Earth moves around the sun. For these reasons, Earth has different seasons.

light from the sun

North America

South America

Earth Orbits the Sun

Earth moves in an **orbit**, or a path, around the sun. It takes Earth one year to orbit the sun. As Earth orbits the sun, the seasons change. A **season** is a time of the year that has a certain kind of weather.

Earth

fall

sun

winter

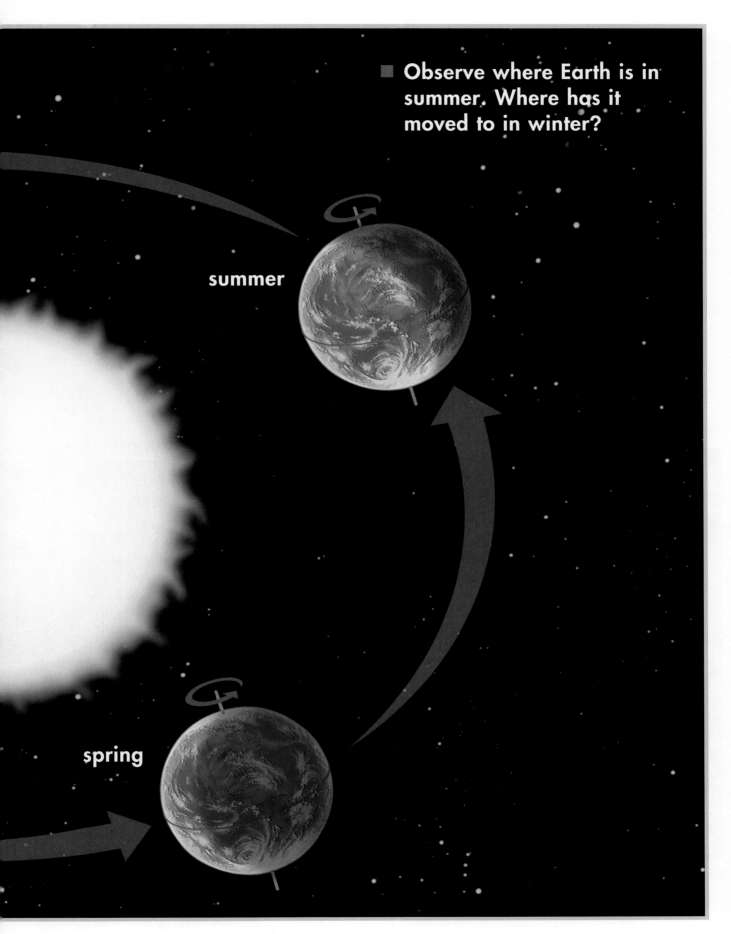

■ Observe where Earth is in summer. Where has it moved to in winter?

summer

spring

Why the Seasons Change

Earth is always tilted in the same direction. When Earth is on one side of the sun, part of Earth faces the sun directly and gets more direct sunlight. This part of Earth has summer.

■ **Is the tilt of Earth the same or different in spring and summer?**

spring

summer

When Earth moves to the other side of the sun, Earth still tilts in the same direction. Now the tilt causes this same part of Earth to face the sun on a slant. Sunlight does not hit Earth as directly. This part of Earth has winter.

Think About It

1. How does Earth move around the sun?

2. Why do the seasons change?

fall

winter

How Does the Moon Move and Change?

Light from the Moon

You will need

foam ball   foil   pencil   flashlight

1 With a partner, cover the ball with foil. Push the pencil into it to make a handle.

2 Observe how the ball looks in the dark. Draw it.

3 Hold the ball by the handle. Have your partner shine the flashlight on the ball. Draw and compare.

Science Skill
When you compare, you tell how two things are alike and different.

Moonlight

The **moon** is the object that appears the largest in the night sky. It seems to shine, but the moon does not really give off its own light. The light from the moon, or **moonlight**, comes from the sun.

moon

The Moon

The moon is a huge ball of rock that orbits Earth. It takes about 29 days for the moon to orbit Earth.

When we look at the moon, it seems to have spots. Some spots are holes called craters. A **crater** is made when a large rock moving through space hits the moon.

■ **Which part of the moon is lighted by the sun?**

Earth

moon

sun

crater

Astronauts explore space and have gone to the moon. They have seen the craters and the gray dust that covers the moon. They have brought moon rocks back to Earth. Astronaut David Scott commanded the *Apollo 15* mission to the moon.

■ **What do you think this astronaut saw?**

The Moon Seems to Change Shape

The moon's orbit makes the moon seem to change shape. At the start of the moon's orbit, the moon is between the sun and Earth. The sun shines directly on the part of the moon that faces it. The part facing us on Earth is dark.

In one week, the moon is one-fourth, or one-quarter, of the way through its orbit. From Earth the moon looks like a half-circle.

In two weeks, the moon is halfway around its orbit. Now Earth is between the sun and the moon. From Earth the moon looks like a full circle.

In three weeks, the moon is three-fourths of the way around again. In four weeks, the moon is back where it started.

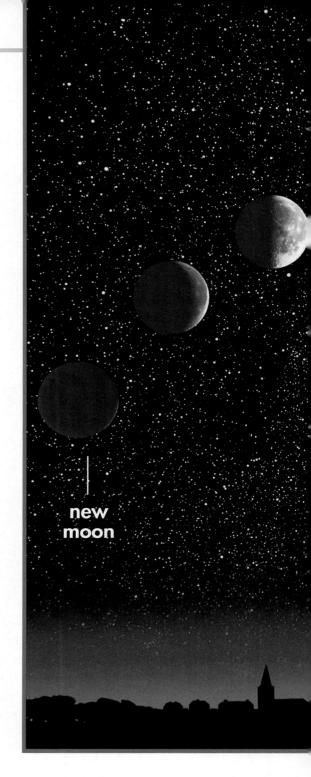

new moon

■ **Why can't we see the new moon?**

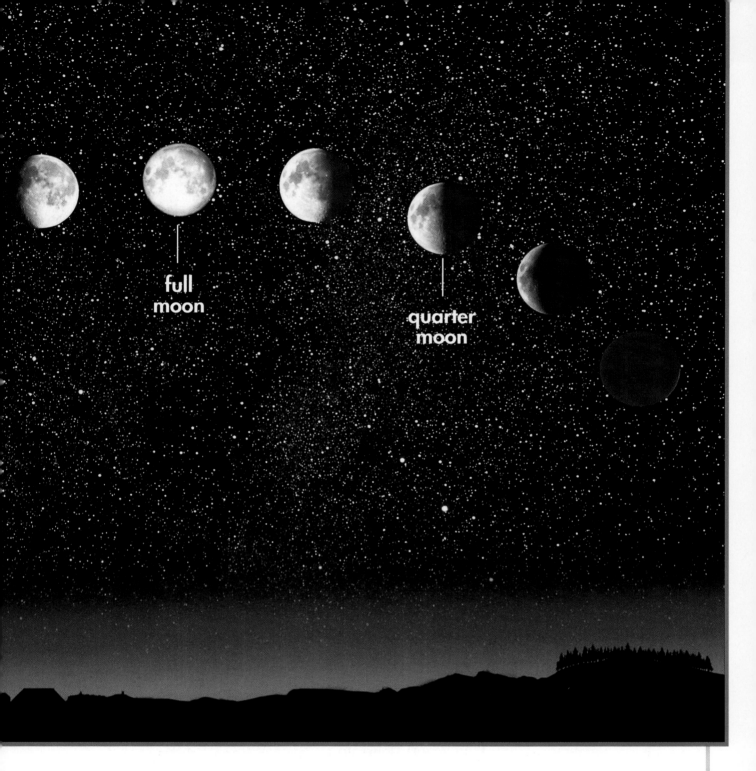

full
moon

quarter
moon

Think About It

1. What makes the moon seem to shine?
2. Why does the moon seem to change shape?

Math Link

Use a Calendar

Most places on Earth have four seasons. Each season begins on about the same day every year. Most calendars show the date when each season begins.

Write

Make a chart like this one. Look at a calendar to find when each season begins. Write the date. Then look at the diagram on pages D20 and D21. Draw a picture in your chart to show where Earth is in relation to the sun in each season. Write sentences to explain your chart.

Where Earth Is in Different Seasons		
Season	When It Begins	Where Earth Is
spring		☼
summer		☼
fall		☼
winter		☼

Social Studies Link

Finding the North Star

For hundreds of years, sailors used stars to find their way. The most important star for them was the North Star. Sailors knew that when they looked at the North Star, they were facing north.

Think and Do

Find the North Star the same way sailors did. First, look at the Big Dipper in the picture.

Big Dipper

Little Dipper

Next, find the two stars on the front of its cup. They line up with the Little Dipper. Last, find the bright star at the end of the handle of the Little Dipper. That is the North Star.

Tell What You Know

1. Use the picture to tell about the moon and why it seems to change shape. Use the words *sun, moonlight, moon,* and *crater*.

Vocabulary

Use the words to tell about each picture.

2.

sun
solar system
solar energy

3.

rotation

4.

planet
orbit
season

5.

star
constellation

Using Science Skills

6. **Compare** Think about summer and winter where you live. Is it warmer in summer or in winter? Are there more hours of daylight in summer or in winter? How do you know?

   Write three sentences that compare summer and winter. You may draw pictures, too.

7. **Use Time/Space Relationships** The moon orbits Earth in about 29 days. As the moon moves, it seems to change shape. Choose three pictures of the moon from pages D28 and D29. For each one, draw a picture to show where the sun, the moon, and Earth are when the moon looks that way.

CHAPTER 2

Earth's Weather

Vocabulary

weather

water cycle

evaporate

water vapor

thermometer

temperature

stratus

cirrus

cumulus

thunderstorm

tornado

hurricane

blizzard

Did You Know?

The highest **temperature** recorded in the United States was 134°F (about 57°C) in Death Valley, California, on July 10, 1913.

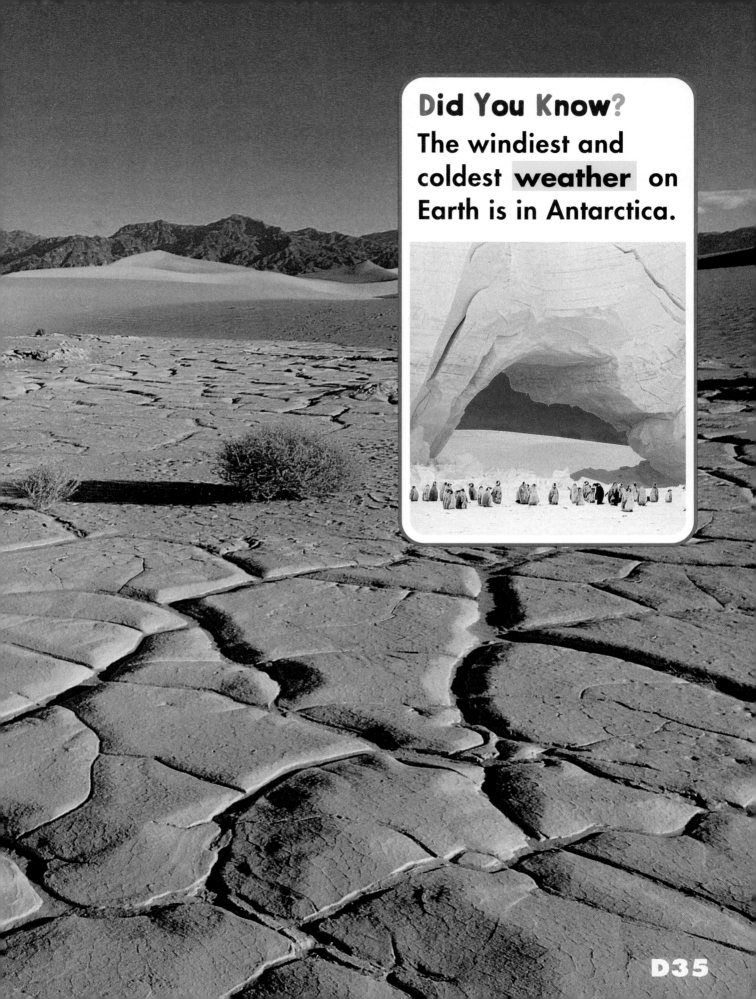

Did You Know?

The windiest and coldest **weather** on Earth is in Antarctica.

How Does Weather Change?

 Investigate

Changes in the Weather

You will need

paper

markers

Weather	
Monday	
Tuesday	
Wednesday	
Thursday	
Friday	

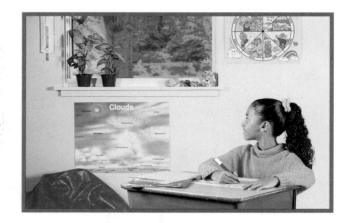

1 Make a weather chart like the one above.

2 Observe the weather each day. Record what you observe.

3 What kinds of weather changes did you observe? Share your information.

Science Skill
When you observe weather, you can use sight, hearing, smell, and touch.

Changes in Weather

What the air is like outside is **weather**. The air may be warm or cool. It may also be rainy, sunny, windy, or cloudy. Weather can change quickly.

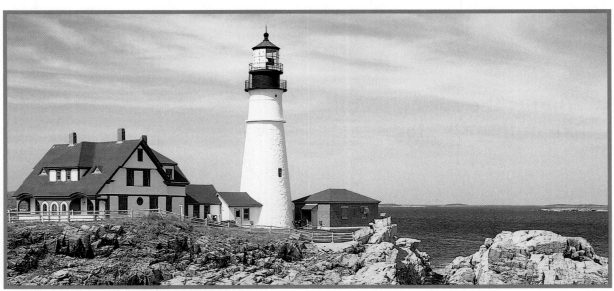

Spring

In many places, the weather changes from season to season. In spring the air gets warmer. In some places, spring is rainy, too. The warmer, wetter weather helps plants grow new leaves and flowers.

■ **What is the spring weather like in these pictures?**

Summer

Summer is the warmest time of the year. Summer days are often hot and sunny. In some places, storms make the weather change quickly.

■ **How might the weather change here? How do you know?**

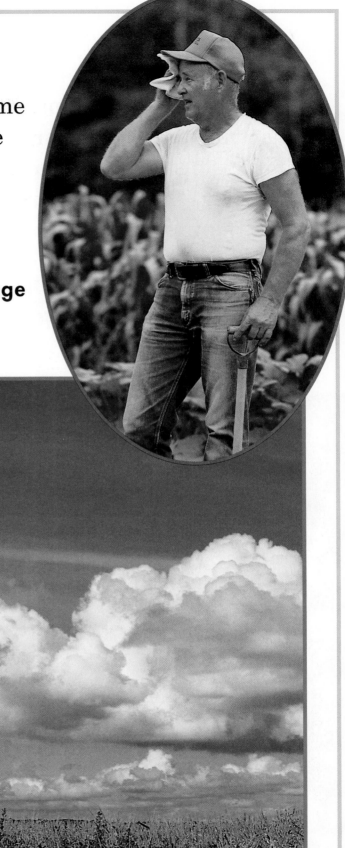

Fall

In fall the air gets cooler. Some fall days are cloudy, but others are sunny and clear. In fall the leaves of some trees change color and then drop off. Some plants die.

■ **How is the weather different on these fall days?**

Winter

Winter is the coldest time of the year. In many places, it gets cold enough for snow. In these places, many trees and bushes have bare branches.

In other places, it cools down just a little in winter. These places may rarely have snow. Many trees there stay green, and flowers keep growing.

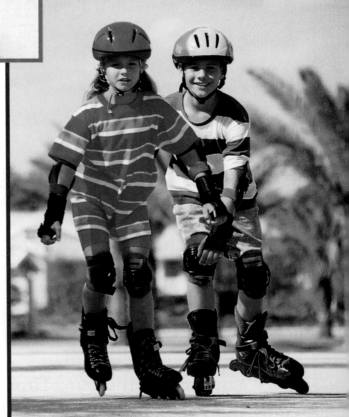

Think About It

1. How does the weather change from day to day?
2. How does the weather change from season to season?

What Is the Water Cycle?

Investigate

Water in the Air

You will need

2 zip-top bags

colored water

tape

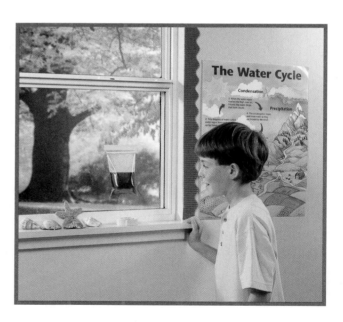

1 Fill each bag halfway with water. Zip the bags closed.

2 Tape one bag to a window in the sun. Tape the other bag to a window in the shade.

3 After 30 minutes, observe both bags. Which bag shows more change?

4 Infer what caused the change.

Science Skill

When you infer, you think about what you observed and figure out what happened.

The Water Cycle

Water moves from the air to the land and back to the air. The way water keeps doing this over and over is called the **water cycle**.

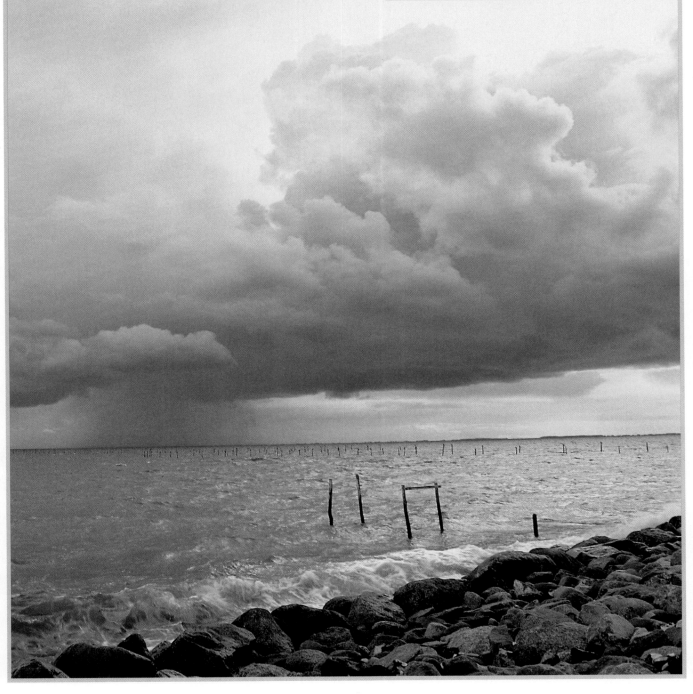

How the Water Cycle Works

4 The drops of water come together and form clouds.

3 The water vapor condenses, or changes into tiny drops of water.

2 This gas, or **water vapor**, meets cool air.

1 The sun's heat makes water **evaporate**, or change into a gas.

ocean

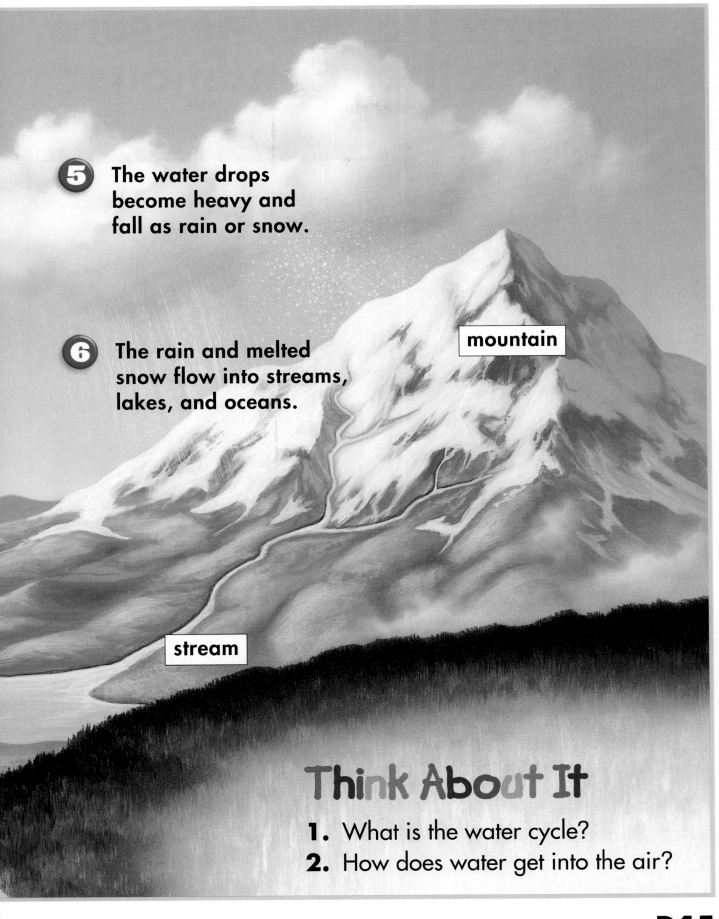

5 The water drops become heavy and fall as rain or snow.

6 The rain and melted snow flow into streams, lakes, and oceans.

mountain

stream

Think About It

1. What is the water cycle?

2. How does water get into the air?

How Do We Measure Weather Conditions?

Investigate

Temperature Outside

You will need

thermometer

paper and pencil

Temperature	
Monday	
Tuesday	
Wednesday	
Thursday	
Friday	

1 Make a chart like this one.

2 At the same time each day, read the thermometer. Record the temperature.

3 Use your data to answer these questions. Did the temperature go up? down? What pattern do you see?

Science Skill
You can use data to look for a pattern of temperature change.

Measuring Weather Conditions

Weather conditions can be measured with tools. Some tools tell how hot the air is. Others tell how fast the wind is blowing or how much rain has fallen.

How Scientists Measure Weather Conditions

Scientists called meteorologists use tools to measure weather conditions. A **thermometer** measures temperature. **Temperature** is a measure of how hot or cold the air is. Scientists use rain gauges to measure how much rain or snow has fallen.

An anemometer measures how fast the wind is blowing. A wind vane shows which way the wind is blowing. It points to the direction the wind is coming from.

thermometers

wind vane

■ **What is the temperature on each thermometer?**

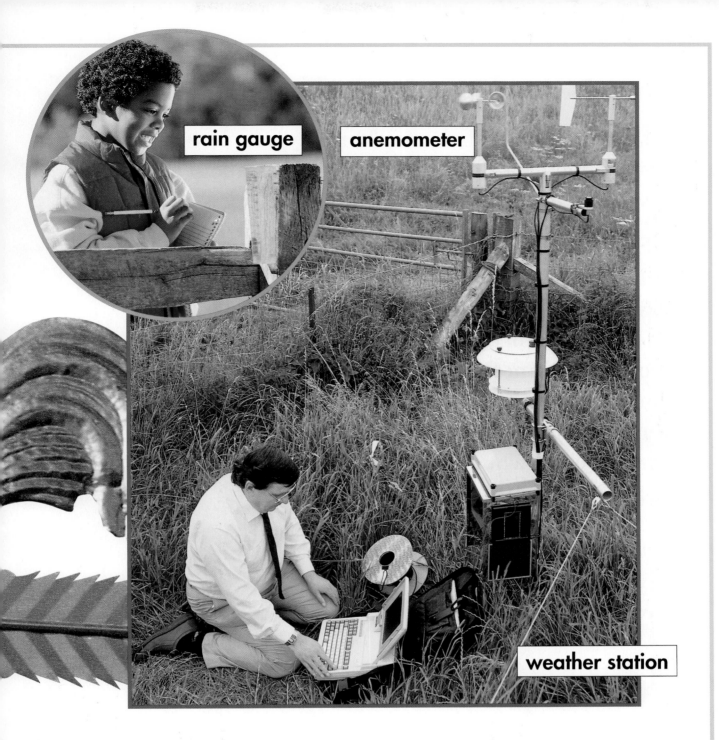

rain gauge

anemometer

weather station

Measuring weather conditions helps people know how to dress when they go outside. It also helps scientists see patterns and predict the weather. They can tell people to get ready if a big storm is on the way.

Clouds and the Weather

Looking at clouds is another way people predict the weather. Clouds give clues about how the weather may change.

Stratus, cirrus, and cumulus are three kinds of clouds. The low, gray clouds that stretch across the sky are **stratus** clouds. They usually bring rain or snow. The thin, feathery clouds high in the sky are **cirrus** clouds. We may see cirrus clouds when the weather is sunny.

stratus clouds

■ **What kind of weather will the stratus clouds bring?**

cumulus clouds

cirrus clouds

The clouds that look like puffy, white cotton are **cumulus** clouds. We see them in fair weather. When cumulus clouds pile up and turn dark, they can bring a storm.

Think About It

1. How can we measure weather conditions?
2. How can clouds help us predict the weather?

How Can We Prepare For Weather?

Clothing for Different Kinds of Weather

You will need

weather picture cards

clothing picture cards

1 With a partner, classify clothing by the weather for which it is used. Place the weather cards face up. Put the clothing cards face down in a pile.

2 Look at a clothing card. Place it under the weather card it belongs with.

3 Take turns until you have classified all the clothing.

Science Skill
When you classify the cards, you put them in groups that show how they are alike.

Preparing for Weather

Weather changes from day to day. It is important to wear clothing that is right for the weather. On some days the weather is stormy. It is important to be prepared for stormy weather.

Hot, Cold, Sunny, Rainy

The right clothing can keep you warm on cold days and cool on hot days. They can keep you dry on rainy days and protect your skin on sunny days.

Hot Day

- Wear loose, light clothing.
- Drink plenty of water.
- Stay indoors or in the shade.

Cold Day

- Wear layers of dark clothing.
- Wear mittens and a hat.
- Keep your skin dry.

The sun can hurt your skin, but you can protect yourself. On a rainy day you can wear things to stay dry.

Sunny Day

- Use sunscreen.
- Wear a hat with a brim.
- Wear sunglasses.

- Why is the girl putting on sunscreen?

Rainy Day

- Wear a raincoat.
- Wear a rain hat or use an umbrella.
- Wear rain boots.

Storms

A **thunderstorm** has rain, thunder, and lightning. Lightning can strike tall things like trees and telephone poles.

Thunderstorm

- Stay away from water.
- Stay away from electricity.
- If you are caught outdoors, stay away from trees and lie down.

A **tornado** is a funnel-shaped cloud. A tornado spins very fast. Its strong winds can destroy buildings.

Tornado

- Listen to television and radio warnings.
- Go to a sheltered place.
- If you are caught outdoors, lie down in a low place.

Hurricane

- Bring loose items inside.
- Cover windows with plywood.
- Go to a sheltered place.

A **hurricane** has strong winds, high ocean waves, and heavy rain. It can cause floods and destroy trees and buildings.

A **blizzard** is a storm with heavy snow and strong winds. It may be hard to see outside.

Blizzard

- Wear layers of clothing.
- Listen to radio warnings.
- If you can't see, follow a fence or something else you can touch.

Think About It

1. How should you dress for cold, sunny weather?
2. How are a tornado and a hurricane different?

Math Link

Measure Rain

This rain gauge measures how much rain falls. It is used by meteorologists, or weather scientists, at the National Weather Service. The gauge has a bottle that collects rain. It also has a ruler that measures how many inches of rain fall.

A meteorologist checks the rain gauge every day and puts the data into a computer. Then newspapers and television stations use this information for their weather reports.

Think and Do

Measure how much rain falls. Make a rain gauge like this one. Put your rain gauge outside in an open area before it rains. When the rain stops, read it. The ruler will show how much rain fell. Record and report your data.

A Poem About Weather

Poets use words to make pictures in the minds of their readers. These word pictures are poems. A poet named Robert Louis Stevenson wrote this poem.

Rain

The rain is raining all around,
It falls on field and tree,
It rains on the umbrellas here,
And on the ships at sea.

Write

Write a poem about the kind of weather you like best. Use the picture in your mind to help you choose words. Read your poem to a classmate. Can your classmate see the picture your poem makes?

Tell What You Know

1. Tell what you know. Use the words *tornado, thunderstorm, hurricane,* and *blizzard.*

Vocabulary

Use the words to complete the sentences.

cirrus	**stratus**	**evaporate**
water cycle	**weather**	**temperature**
thermometer	**cumulus**	**water vapor**

2. What the air outside is like is _____.

3. Heat makes water _____, or change into a gas.

4. A _____ measures the _____, or how hot or cold the air is.

5. Three kinds of clouds are _____, _____, and _____.

6. The way water moves from the land to the air and back again is called the _____.

7. When water evaporates, it changes into _____.

Using Science Skills

8. **Observe/Predict** Look out a window at the clouds. What kind of clouds are they? What kind of weather do you think is coming? On a sheet of paper, write what you predict. The next day, see if you were correct.

    Use clouds to predict the weather for five days in a row. How many times were you correct?

9. **Observe/Collect Data** Look outside each day for five days. Observe how hard the wind is blowing. Then use the pictures to find out what kind of wind it is. Record your data in a chart.

| no wind | breeze | wind | strong wind |

Trace Your Shadow

1. On a sunny morning, ask a partner to use chalk to trace your shadow on a sidewalk.

2. Write the time of day on your shadow, and predict how your shadow will look later in the day.

3. In the afternoon, trace a new shadow. Compare.

Which Paper Towel Dries First?

1. With a family member or a classmate, wet three paper towels.

2. Put each towel in a different place.

3. Predict which towel will dry first.

4. Check the towels every 15 minutes. Which one dries first? last? Why?

Observe the Night Sky

1. With an adult family member, go outside on a clear night.

2. Find the moon. What shape does it have?

3. Draw pictures of what you observe.

4. Do the activity again in one week.

5. Communicate how your pictures are different and why.

Make Sun Prints

1. Cut two shapes from construction paper.

2. Place the shapes on black paper.

3. With an adult, go outside. Leave one sheet of black paper in the shade and the other one in the sun.

4. After several hours, remove the cutouts from the black paper. Observe. Why do you think this happens?

National Air and Space Museum, Washington, D.C.

At this museum, you can learn about space and our solar system. You can see exhibits of some of the spacecraft used to explore space.

Plan Your Own Expedition

Visit a space exhibit or a museum near you. Or log on to The Learning Site.

GO ONLINE   www.harcourtschool.com

Science in Indiana

Exploring Matter

Indianapolis Museum of Art

In this unit you will learn about matter and how it changes. People change matter when they paint, draw, sculpt, and make shapes from clay.

Indianapolis

The Indianapolis Museum of Art has 42,000 pieces of art. It is one of the finest art museums in the United States. It has works by artists from Indiana and around the world.

Indianapolis Museum of Art

The museum has paintings, sculptures, prints, drawings, and photographs. Ceramics, rugs, fabrics, and costumes are also among the artworks at the museum. The colors, textures, and variety of shapes help make each piece of art at the museum special.

Each year many people visit the Indianapolis Museum of Art. They enjoy looking at art and learning about it. Children and adults can even take classes so they can learn to make their own artworks.

wall hanging from Morocco

Think About It

1. Why do people visit the Indianapolis Museum of Art?

2. What is your favorite kind of art? Why?

Art Link

Make a Sculpture

Use building blocks or an erector set to make a sculpture. Display your sculpture and describe it to your classmates. What are some of the parts of the sculpture?

Math Link

Which Is the Tallest?

Observe the sculptures your classmates made for the Art Link. Tell which sculpture you think is the tallest. Everyone in class will probably not agree. Discuss your observations with your classmates. If everyone still does not agree, use rulers to measure the sculptures. See which sculpture is the tallest.

Exploring Matter

UNIT EXPERIMENT

Water and Rusting

As you do this unit, you will find out how objects change. Plan and do a test to find out how water helps make some objects rust.

CHAPTER 1

Observing and Measuring Matter

Vocabulary

matter
property
mass
solid
centimeter
liquid
milliliter
gas

Did You Know?
A **gas** called propane is burned to heat the air in a hot-air balloon.

Did You Know?
A **solid** that weighs 100 pounds on Earth would weigh only 17 pounds on the moon.

What Is Matter?

 Investigate

Matter

You will need

3 balls or markers

paper and pencil

1 Observe how the objects are alike and different.

2 Think of ways to classify the objects. Write your ideas.

3 Choose one way to classify the objects into groups.

4 Explain to a classmate how you classified the objects.

Science Skill
When you classify, you look for ways that things are alike. Then you put the things that are alike into a group.

Matter

Matter is what all things are made of. Trees, milk, and air are all made of matter. Even you are made of matter! What different kinds of matter do you see here?

Forms of Matter

Matter has three forms. It can be a solid, a liquid, or a gas. The party hats, the bowl, the cups, and the chair are solids. The juice is a liquid. The air in the balloons is a gas.

solids

■ **How are the objects on these two pages alike and different?**

liquid

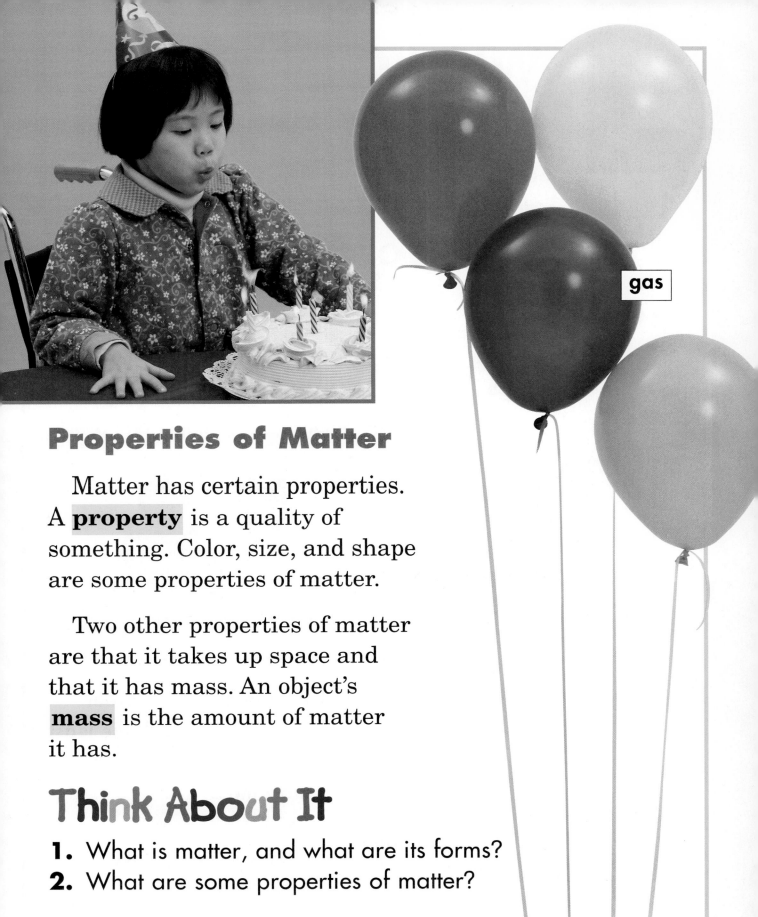

gas

Properties of Matter

Matter has certain properties. A **property** is a quality of something. Color, size, and shape are some properties of matter.

Two other properties of matter are that it takes up space and that it has mass. An object's **mass** is the amount of matter it has.

Think About It

1. What is matter, and what are its forms?

2. What are some properties of matter?

What Can We Find Out About Solids?

Solids

You will need

4 objects

balance

paper and pencil

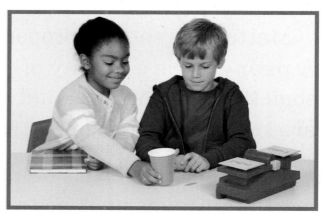

1 Use the balance to find the mass of each object.

2 Put the objects in order from the one with the least mass to the one with the most mass.

3 Make a chart that shows the objects in order from the one with the least mass to the one with the most mass.

Science Skill

When you put objects in order, you can arrange them from least to most.

Solids

A solid is one kind of matter. Like all matter, it takes up space and has mass. A **solid** is the only form of matter that has a shape of its own.

Finding Out About Solids

All the objects you see here are solids. They are different in color, size, and shape. Some of the objects are hard. Others are soft. They have different textures.

Solids are alike in some important ways. Each one has its own size and shape. A solid will not change in size or shape unless you do something such as cut, bend, or break it.

■ **How are these objects alike and different?**

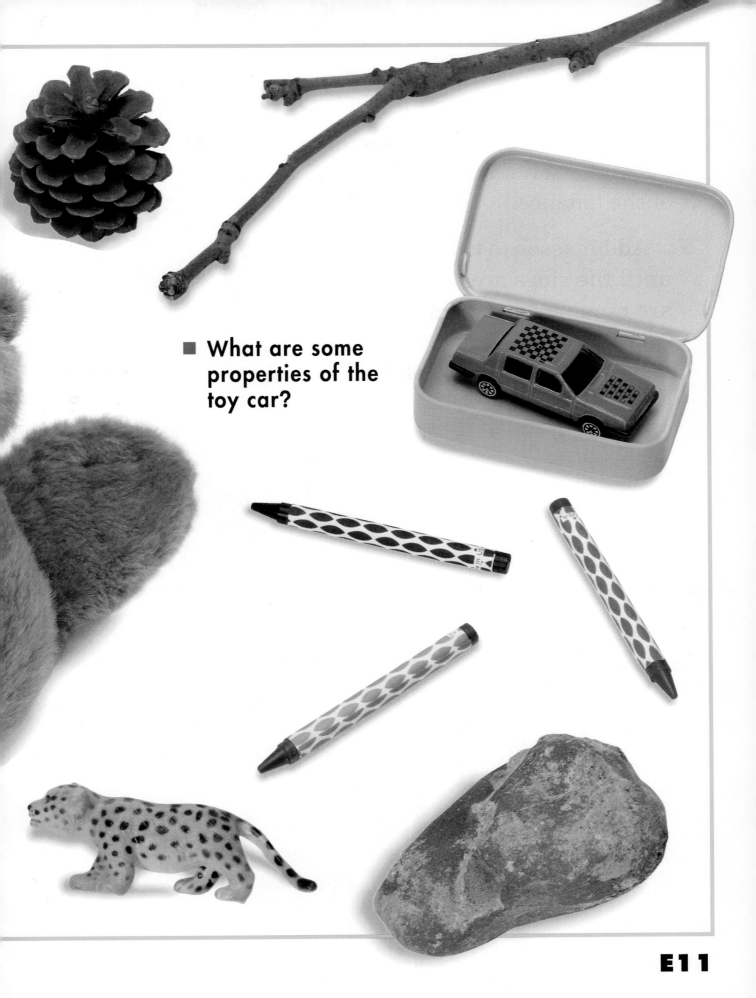

■ What are some
properties of the
toy car?

Measuring Solids

A balance can help you find out the mass of a solid. Put the solid on one side of the balance.

Add masses to the other side until the sides are even. There are numbers on the masses. Add them to find how much mass equals the mass of the solid.

■ **What is this girl using to measure the mass of the toy?**

You can measure how long or wide a solid is. You can also measure how big around it is.

A **centimeter** is a unit used to measure length. You can use centimeters to find the length of a solid.

■ **What are the boy and the girl using to measure the objects?**

centimeter

How Many Centimeters Long?	
Object	Number of Centimeters
box	28
wood	27

Think About It

1. How are all solids alike?

2. How can you measure the length of a solid?

What Can We Find Out About Liquids?

Liquids

You will need

marker

3 colors of water

 measuring cup

 3 containers

1. Draw a line at the same height on all 3 containers. Pour water into each container to the line.

2. Pour the water from one container into the measuring cup. Measure, and record the number from the cup.

3. Repeat Step 2 for the other containers.

4. Compare the numbers. What can you infer?

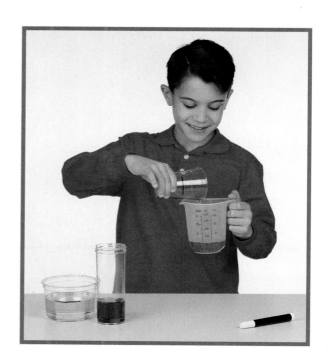

Science Skill

You can use a measuring cup to measure the amount of a liquid.

Liquids

A **liquid** is a form of matter that does not have its own shape. It flows to take the shape of its container. Like a solid, a liquid takes up space and has mass. You can see and feel a liquid.

Finding Out About Liquids

The liquid in a bottle has the same shape as the bottle. As you tilt the bottle, the liquid changes shape. If the liquid is poured from the bottle into a glass, it takes the shape of the glass.

■ **What shape has the honey taken?**

A liquid does not change in amount unless you add more or take some away. If you pour it into a glass, the amount of liquid stays the same.

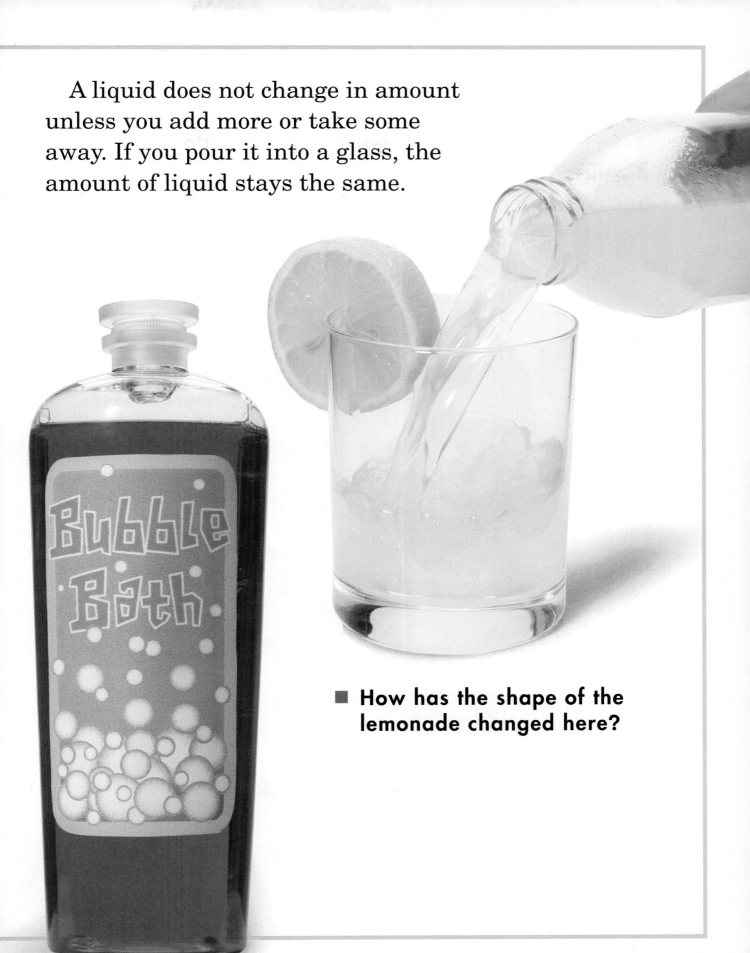

■ **How has the shape of the lemonade changed here?**

Measuring Liquids

Like solids, liquids have mass. A container with liquid in it has more mass than the same container with no liquid. You can measure the mass of a liquid by putting it on a pan balance.

■ **Which cup has more mass? How do you know?**

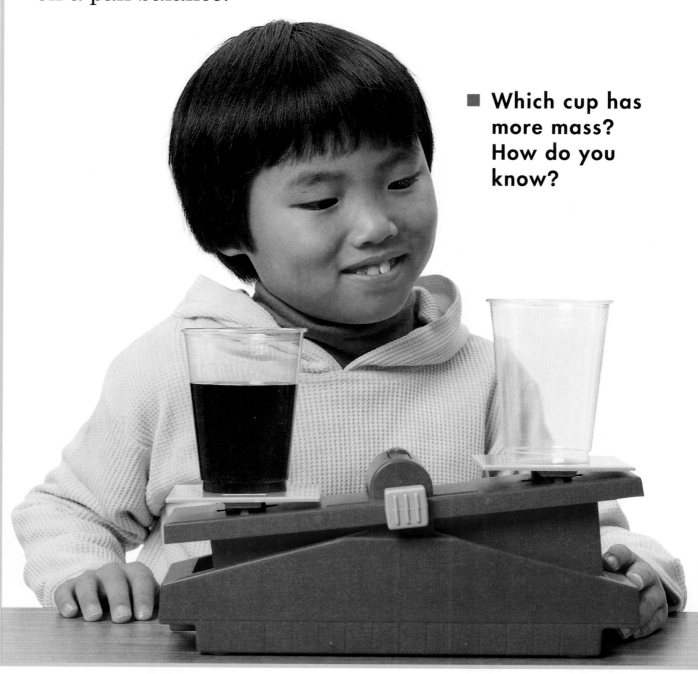

You can also measure the volume of a liquid. Volume is the amount of space a liquid takes up. A **milliliter** is a unit used to measure the volume of a liquid.

Volume in Milliliters	
Liquid	Number of Milliliters
apple juice	75 milliliters
orange juice	150 milliliters

Think About It

1. What are two properties of liquids?
2. How can you measure a liquid?

What Can We Find Out About Gases?

Gases

You will need

water   cup   paper towel

1 Push a paper towel tightly into the bottom of the cup.

2 Turn the cup upside down. Push it straight down in the water.

3 Observe the cup. Is there water in it? Lift the cup straight up out of the water.

4 Infer what happened.

Science Skill
When you infer, you use what you know and what you observe to explain what happened.

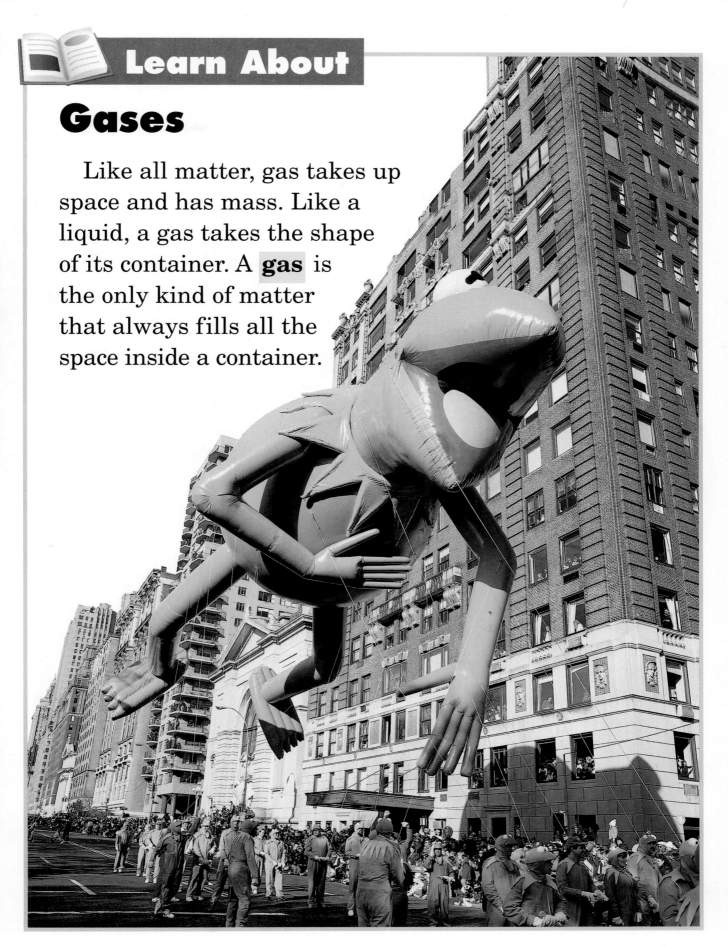

Gases

Like all matter, gas takes up space and has mass. Like a liquid, a gas takes the shape of its container. A **gas** is the only kind of matter that always fills all the space inside a container.

The Shapes Gases Take

When you pump air into a soccer ball, the air spreads out inside. It fills the space of its container. The air takes the round shape of the ball.

■ **What shape is the air inside the bubble?**

Air

Air is made up of gases and is all around you. You often cannot see or feel air, but you can see what it does. Air can lift a kite and fill a swimming float.

■ **How is this girl using air?**

Measuring Gases

Like all matter, gases have mass. You can measure the mass of a gas by tying balloons to the ends of a rod. A balloon filled with air is heavier than a balloon just like it with no air.

■ **How do you know the balloon filled with air is heavier?**

An inventor makes something new to solve a problem. Garrett Morgan was an inventor. He knew some gases were harmful. He invented a gas mask to keep firefighters and others safe from harmful gases.

gas mask

Think About It

1. What is a gas?
2. How can you measure a gas?

Math Link

Find Solid Figures

In math, figures that are not flat are called solids. Spheres, cubes, and cylinders are solid figures. A sphere has the shape of a ball. A cube has the shape of a box. A cylinder has the shape of a can. Many of the solid objects you see have these shapes.

sphere

cube

cylinder

Think and Do

Make a chart. In your classroom, find objects that match the three figures. Draw a picture of each object, and write a label for it.

Solid Figures		
Sphere	Cube	Cylinder
baseball		

Health/Math Link

How Much Liquid Is in Fruit?

Many living things are partly solid and partly liquid. These fruits are solid outside, but inside them is juice—a liquid.

Write

With your teacher, wash and peel fruit, and cut it into rings. Place the rings on a balance. Find and record the mass. Then trace the fruit rings.

Hang the rings in a sunny window. Predict what will happen to the mass. After 5 days, find and record the mass. Trace the fruit rings. Write sentences to tell what you did and whether you predicted correctly.

E27

Tell What You Know

1. What are the properties of each kind of matter?

solid

liquid

gas

Vocabulary

Write the letter of the word that best completes each sentence.

a. gas
b. liquid
c. centimeters
d. solid
e. mass
f. milliliters

2. A _____ fills a balloon.

3. A balance measures the _____ of an object.

4. A _____ takes the shape of a bottle.

5. Liquids may be measured in _____ .

6. An object's length may be measured in _____ .

7. A chair is a _____ because it keeps its shape.

Using Science Skills

8. Classify Make a chart like this one. Then look through old magazines to find pictures that show each kind of matter. Cut out the pictures and glue them in the correct places. Write a label for each picture.

Kinds of Matter		
Solids	Liquids	Gases

9. Measure Choose five small objects to measure. With a centimeter ruler, measure them and record how long each object is. Then put the objects in order from shortest to longest.

CHAPTER 2

Changes in Matter

Vocabulary

mixture
reversible
irreversible

Did You Know?
Mixing salt and water is
reversible. When some
of the water in the Great
Salt Lake dries up, the salt
separates from the water.

Did You Know?
Air is a **mixture** of 11 different gases.

What Happens When You Mix Matter?

 Investigate

Mixing Matter

You will need

plastic knife

nuts, seeds, dried fruit

measuring cup

zip-top bag

1 Cut up the dried fruit. Measure 100 milliliters each of nuts, seeds, and fruit.

2 Put the foods in the bag. Close the bag tightly and shake.

3 Observe. What has changed or not changed?

Science Skill
You can use more than one of your senses to observe something changing.

Cutting and Mixing Matter

Matter can be cut and mixed. When solid matter is cut, its shape changes, but its mass stays the same. When pieces of solid matter are mixed together, each piece stays the same.

Cutting and Shaping Matter

Cutting is just one way you can change matter. This loaf of bread is a solid. It has been cut into slices. The slices have a different shape from the loaf, but they are the same bread. Together, the slices have the same mass as the loaf.

■ **How did the paper change when it was cut? How has it stayed the same?**

If you change just the shape of matter, its mass stays the same. These two pieces of clay were once alike. They had the same shape and the same mass. Then the shape of one piece was changed, but its mass is still the same.

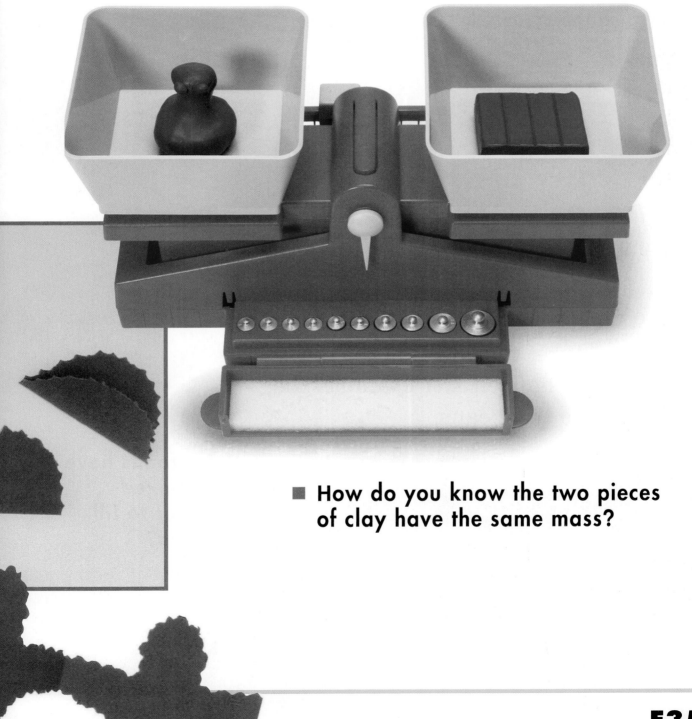

■ **How do you know the two pieces of clay have the same mass?**

Mixing Matter

When you put different kinds of matter together, you make a mixture. A **mixture** is something made up of two or more things. Things you put together in a mixture do not change.

A taco is filled with a mixture of beans, cheese, tomatoes, sauce, and lettuce. If you separate the foods in the mixture, you will find that they have not changed. For example, the beans are still beans.

■ **What foods have been mixed together to fill the taco?**

■ **What kinds of things are in the jar? Why is this a mixture?**

Think About It

1. What happens when you cut and shape matter?
2. What happens when you mix matter together?

LESSON 2

How Can Water Change?

Investigate

One Way That Water Changes

You will need

ice cubes

lamp

cloth

clock

1 Write about some ways to make an ice cube melt faster.

2 Plan an investigation for two of the ways. Follow your plan.

CAUTION Be careful if you use the lamp.

3 Record the time it takes each ice cube to melt.

4 Communicate to a classmate which way melted the ice faster.

Science Skill

You can plan an investigation to see which way works the best.

E38

How Water Can Change

Water can be a solid, a gas, or a liquid. Water as a solid may be ice or snow. Water as a gas is water vapor. In this picture, heat from the Earth is changing water from one form to another.

geysers,
Yellowstone National Park

Adding Heat Changes Water

Adding heat can make water change from one form of matter to another. Ice is water in its solid form. Water is a solid only when its temperature is 0°C or lower.

Adding heat raises the temperature of the ice. If the temperature goes above 0°C, the ice melts, or changes to a liquid.

■ **Why are the icicles melting?**

A puddle is liquid water. The sun's heat may cause the water in the puddle to evaporate, or change to water vapor.

When water gets hot enough, it boils, like the water in a kettle. When water boils, it evaporates.

■ **What makes liquid water turn into a gas?**

Taking Away Heat Changes Water

Taking away heat, or cooling, can also change the form of water. When enough heat is taken away from water, it freezes, or becomes a solid called ice. When enough heat is taken away from water vapor, it condenses, or becomes liquid. Drops of liquid water form clouds and may fall as rain.

■ **How did the cloud form?**

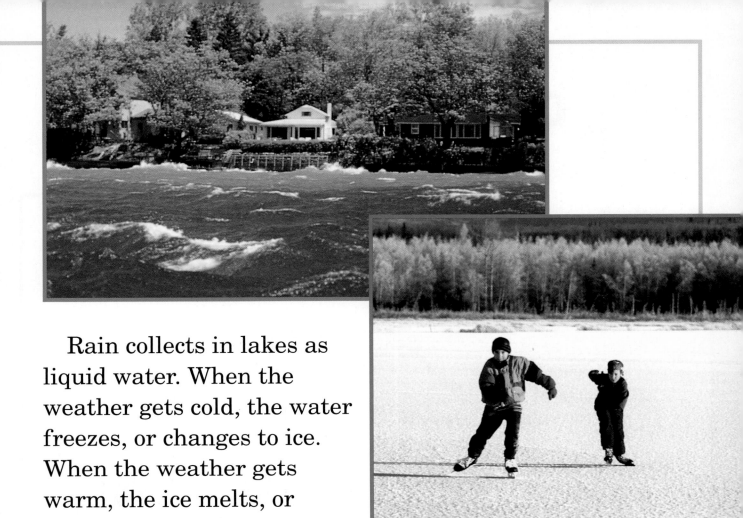

Rain collects in lakes as liquid water. When the weather gets cold, the water freezes, or changes to ice. When the weather gets warm, the ice melts, or changes to liquid water.

■ **How did the water in this lake change?**

Water changes from liquid to ice and back, and from liquid to vapor and back. All these changes are reversible. In a **reversible** change, matter can be changed back to the way it was.

Think About It

1. What are the three forms of water?

2. What can make water change its form?

LESSON 3

What Other Ways Does Matter Change?

A Mixture

You will need

½ cup of warm water

spoon

salt

pan

1 Mix one spoonful of salt into the water. Stir well.

2 Pour the salt-and-water mixture into the pan.

3 Put the pan in a warm place. Predict what will happen.

4 Observe in two days. Did you predict correctly?

Science Skill

When you predict, you use what you know to make a good guess.

Other Ways Matter Changes

Matter can change in different ways. Some changes are reversible. Other changes are not reversible. How has the matter in this pizza changed?

Mixing and Shaping

You can mix together some things and then separate them again. Each thing will still be the same as it was before.

- **Why is this mixture reversible?**

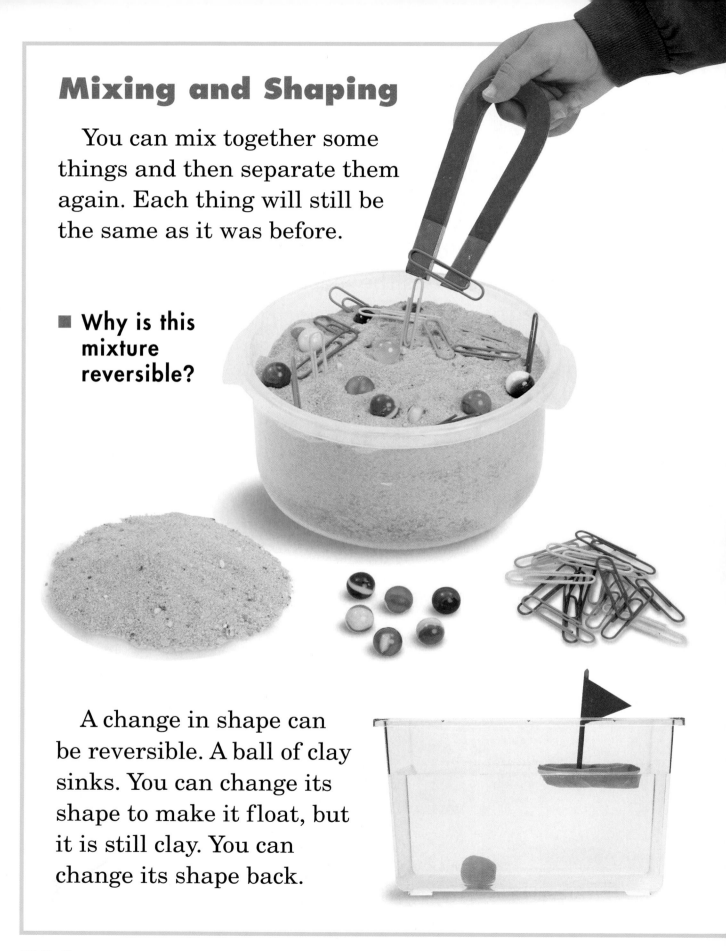

A change in shape can be reversible. A ball of clay sinks. You can change its shape to make it float, but it is still clay. You can change its shape back.

Gelatin must be changed before it is ready to eat. First, the solid powder is mixed with hot water. When the hot liquid mixture cools, it becomes firm. If the gelatin is heated, it begins to change back. Some of the gelatin melts and becomes liquid again.

■ How can a gelatin dessert change?

Burning, Cooking, and Rusting

Some changes to matter are **irreversible**, or not able to be changed back. In an irreversible change, matter cannot be changed back to the way it once was. Fire and high heat often cause irreversible changes.

Burning causes wood to change to ashes, gases, and smoke. The ashes, gases, and smoke cannot be changed back to wood again.

■ What irreversible change will this fire cause?

Cooking can also cause irreversible changes. Cooking makes an egg change from a liquid to a solid. It also changes the egg's color, texture, and taste. A cooked egg cannot become raw, or uncooked, again.

■ **How did the egg change?**

Another irreversible change is rusting. Iron in metal rusts when it mixes with water and air. When iron rusts, it cannot be changed back to the way it was before.

unchanged iron nails

rusted iron nails

Think About It

1. What are some changes in matter that are reversible?
2. What are some changes in matter that are irreversible?

Math Link

How Much Liquid Changes to a Gas?

You can use a measuring cup to find out how much liquid water changes into a gas.

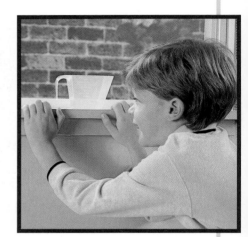

Write

Pour 100 mL of water into a measuring cup. Put the cup on a windowsill in the sun.

After three days, measure and record how much water is in the cup. Write a subtraction story to figure out how much of the water evaporated, or changed to a gas.

A Potter Changes the Shape of Matter

A potter uses clay to make beautiful things. This potter is shaping clay into a pot. He will put the clay pot in a very hot oven. The clay will change to a different kind of matter that is very hard. Some kinds of clay can get hard just by drying in the air.

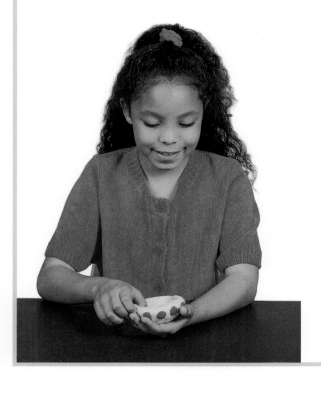

Think and Do

Make a pot from clay. Work the clay into a shape. Try using different colors of clay to make your pot more interesting.

Tell What You Know

1. Tell how matter is being changed in each picture.

Vocabulary

Tell which picture answers each question.

2. Which picture shows an *irreversible* change?

3. Which picture shows a *mixture*?

4. Which picture shows a *reversible* change?

a.

b.

c.

Using Science Skills

5. Plan and Conduct a Simple Investigation/Predict Plan a way to show how water can change from a liquid to a solid and back to a liquid. List the materials you will need. Draw pictures to show each step you will take. Predict what will happen, and then follow your plan. Did you predict correctly?

6. Observe/Classify Look at pictures in magazines. Find three kinds of foods that are mixtures. Then make a chart like this one. Write the name of each mixture. Then list the foods that make up each one.

Food Mixtures		
Mixture 1 _____	Mixture 2 _____	Mixture 3 _____

Activities
for Home or School

The Strength of Air

1. Close a zip-top bag around a straw. Then blow into the straw.

2. Pull out the straw, and quickly finish zipping the bag closed.

3. How many books can you pile on your bag of air? Record what you observe.

4. Does air take up space? Can the air in the bag hold up a lot of books? Share what you observe.

Disappearing Water

1. Pour the same amount of water into two clear cups that are the same size and shape.

2. Use tape to mark the level of water in each cup.

3. Cover one cup with plastic wrap.

4. Leave the cups side by side for a few days.

5. Write about what you observe. What happens to the water in the two cups? Why?

Float or Sink

1. With an adult, fill an aquarium or a pail with water.

2. With the adult, choose a variety of small objects.

3. Make a chart with the headings *Float* and *Sink*.

4. Place the objects one by one into the water.

5. Record in the chart whether each object floats or sinks.

Freeze It

1. With an adult, fill a small empty film container with water. Snap the cover on the container. Place the container in a freezer.

2. Place a block of wood in the freezer.

3. Predict what will happen to each.

4. The next day, remove and observe the water and the block.

5. Compare what happened to the water to what happened to the block of wood.

Robert C. Williams American Museum of Papermaking, Atlanta, Georgia

At this museum, you can learn about paper and how it was invented. You can also see how matter is changed when people make paper.

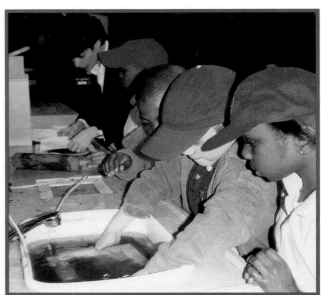

Plan Your Own Expedition

Visit an exhibit or a museum near you. Or log on to The Learning Site.

GO ONLINE www.harcourtschool.com

Science in Indiana

Energy in Motion

Clifty Falls State Park

Madison

In this unit you will learn about forces that make things move. At Clifty Falls State Park in Madison, visitors can see forces of nature at work.

Clifty Falls State Park was named after Big Clifty Falls. This waterfall was formed thousands of years ago during the Ice Age. It began when the flowing waters of Clifty Creek dropped 200 feet into the Ohio River.

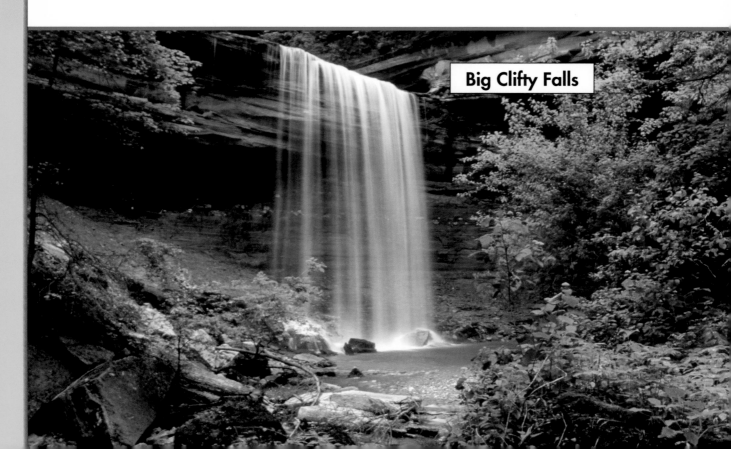

Big Clifty Falls

Now Big Clifty Falls drops 60 feet. Clifty Falls State Park has three other waterfalls. Little Clifty Falls also drops 60 feet. Hoffman Falls drops 78 feet. Tunnel Falls drops 83 feet. Tunnel Falls is the highest waterfall in Indiana.

The park also has an underground tunnel that looks like a cave. The 600-foot tunnel was built about 150 years ago. Today visitors can hike inside the tunnel and use flashlights to have a close look inside.

entrance to the tunnel

Think About It

1. How did the waterfalls form?

2. Why do many visitors like to hike inside the tunnel?

Writing Link

Make a Waterfall

Pile up some rocks in a tub. Use a large plastic cup of water to model a waterfall. Watch the way the waterfall moves. Write one or two sentences about what you observe. Then share your observations with the class.

Math Link

Estimate the Height

Estimate the total of the heights of all four waterfalls at Clifty Falls State Park. Remember that you can round to the nearest ten. After you have an estimate, add the heights to find the total.

Tunnel Falls

Energy in Motion

UNIT EXPERIMENT

Metals and Magnets

As you do this unit, you will find out how magnets work. Plan and do a test to find out what metals a magnet attracts.

Forces and Motion

Vocabulary

force
wind
gravity
magnet
motion

Did You Know?
Cheetahs use **motion** to catch their food. They are the fastest land animals.

Did You Know?

Sometimes **wind** is so strong that it can push a piece of wood into a roof.

What Are Forces?

 Investigate

Pushes and Pulls

You will need

paper and pencil

Pushes and Pulls		
What I Moved	Push	Pull

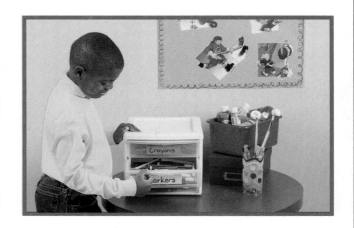

1 Make a chart like this one.

2 Move some objects. Observe how you move them.

3 Ask yourself if you used a push or a pull to move each object. Record your answers.

4 Share with a classmate what you observed.

Science Skill
When you move objects, you can observe pushes and pulls.

Forces

A **force** is a push or a pull that makes something move. These children are trying to get the dog to move. Which child is pushing? Which child is pulling?

Pushes and Pulls

You can push or pull something to change its location, or the place where something is. You can also use a push or a pull to stop something from moving.

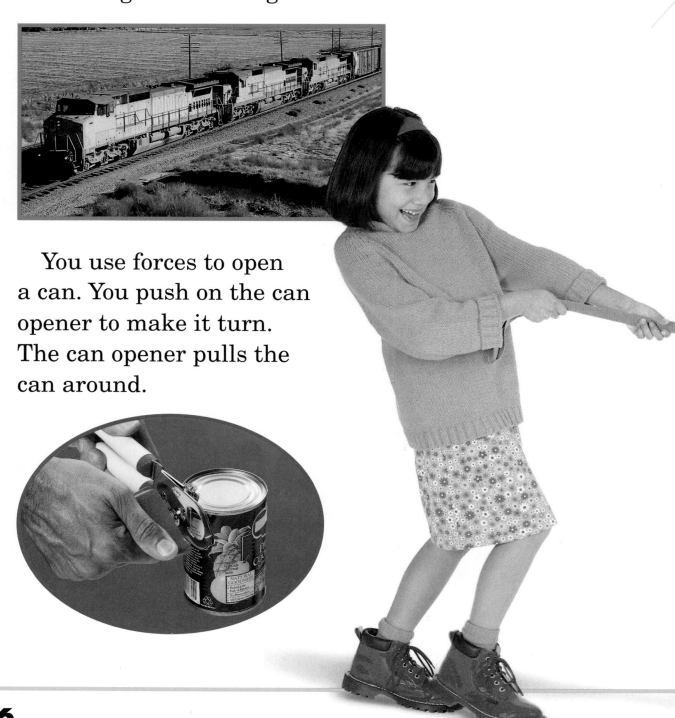

You use forces to open a can. You push on the can opener to make it turn. The can opener pulls the can around.

You use forces to change the direction of a moving object. When you push a ball, you change its location. The ball moves. Your push can also change the direction it is moving in.

■ **Which kind of force is this dog using?**

Change in Direction

A moving object will travel in a straight line if it is not touched. If someone or something pushes the object, its direction can be changed.

straight

zigzag

You can predict how the direction of an object will change. A push on the right side will make an object go to the left. A push on the left side will make an object go to the right.

■ **What changed the direction of the marble?**

back and forth

curved

circular

Kinds of Forces

Moving air is called **wind**. The wind pushes on the sails of a sailboat to help make the boat move.

Moving water also pushes things. You can see and feel the force of water in rivers, streams, and oceans.

■ **How is water moving the raft?**

The force that pulls things toward the center of Earth is called **gravity**. A sled moves down a hill because of gravity. Gravity keeps us on the ground.

Magnetism is also a force. You can use a magnet to pull objects made of iron. Magnets can move iron objects without touching them.

■ What force is the boy using to make the picture?

Think About It

1. What is a force?
2. How can you use forces?

How Do Magnets Work?

Investigate

Magnets

You will need

2 bar magnets   **paper and pencil**

1 Form a hypothesis about what happens when you bring together the ends of two magnets.

Do the Ends Attract or Repel?	
Ends	Attract or Repel?
N end and S end	
S end and N end	
N end and N end	
S end and S end	

2 Bring the *N* end of one magnet toward the *S* end of the other magnet. Record what you observe in a chart like this one.

3 Repeat Step 2, bringing an *S* end toward an *N* end. Repeat, using two *N* ends and then two *S* ends. Record what you observe.

4 Think about what happened. Was your hypothesis correct?

Science Skill

When you form a hypothesis, you say what you think will happen.

Magnets

A **magnet** is a piece of iron or steel that attracts, or pulls, other objects made of iron and steel. Disks made of iron can be held up by the pull of magnets.

Magnets and What They Do

Magnets can be found in nature or made by people. The first magnets were pieces of lodestone, a kind of rock that is a magnet. Magnets made by people may look like balls, horseshoes, rings, bars, wands, and disks.

lodestone

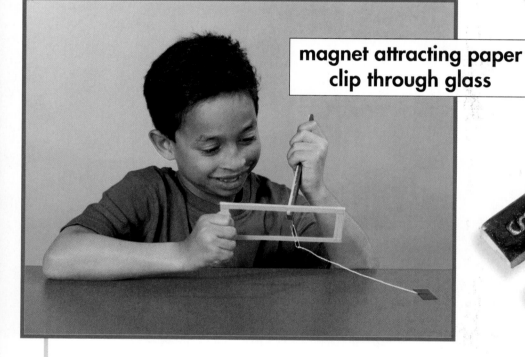

magnet attracting paper clip through glass

A magnet can attract objects even without touching them. It can do this because the magnet's pull can pass through air, water, and some solids.

Magnets have two poles, or ends. One is the north-seeking, or *N*, pole. The other is the south-seeking, or *S*, pole. The pull of a magnet is strongest at the poles and weakest in the middle.

■ **Why are steel balls hanging from the poles of the magnet and not from the middle?**

Opposite poles attract, or pull, each other. The *N* pole of one magnet and the *S* pole of another magnet attract each other. Like poles repel each other, or push each other away. Two *N* poles repel each other, and two *S* poles repel each other.

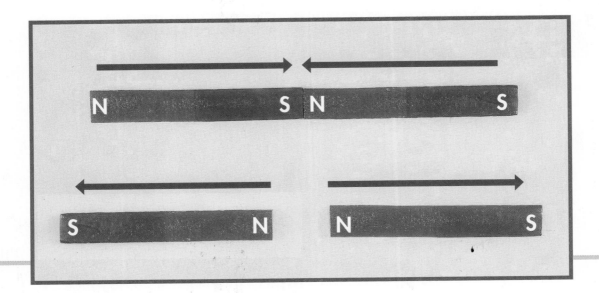

How People Use Magnets

People use magnets in many ways. Magnets are used to hold cabinet doors shut and to hold things to surfaces made of iron or steel. A certain kind of magnet is used in making doorbells, telephones, computers, and televisions.

■ **How are magnets being used in this classroom?**

How Magnets Are Used in Compasses

A magnet is used in making a compass. The magnet is shaped like a needle. It always points to the north. When you know where north is, you can infer where south, east, and west are.

Think About It

1. What happens when you bring the poles of two magnets toward each other?
2. What are some ways magnets are used?

How Can We Measure Motion?

Investigate

One Way to Measure Motion

You will need

board

6 books

meterstick

toy truck

1 Make a low ramp. Let the toy truck roll down.

2 Measure from the bottom of the ramp to where the truck stopped. Record the distance.

3 Make the ramp higher. Then repeat Steps 1 and 2.

4 Use numbers to compare your data. When did the truck go farther? Why?

Science Skill
You can use numbers to find out how far an object moves.

Measuring Motion

Forces can make people and things move. When something moves, it is in **motion**. These people are in motion. What force is making them move?

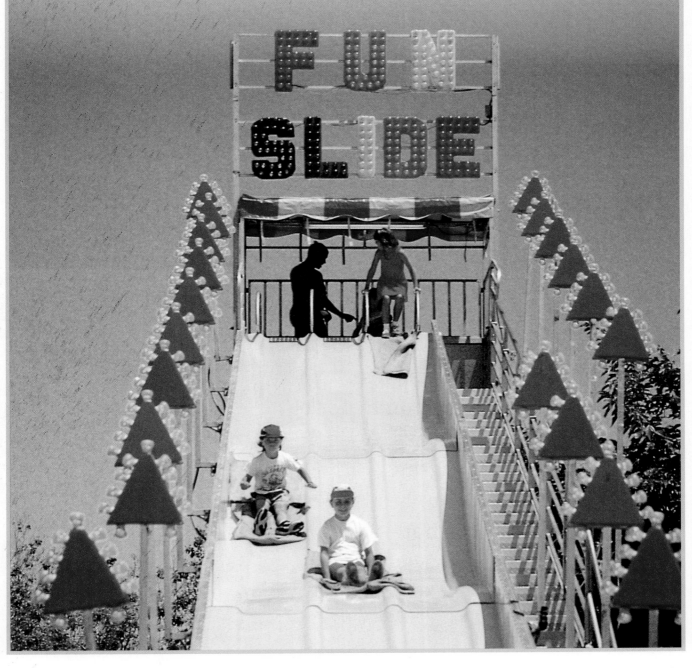

Force and Motion

Something light is easier to move than something heavy. Less force is needed to move light things, and more force is needed to move heavy things.

It also takes less force to move something on a smooth surface than on a rough surface. It takes less force to pull a wagon on a sidewalk than on grass. A rough surface like grass causes more friction. Friction is a force that makes it harder to move things.

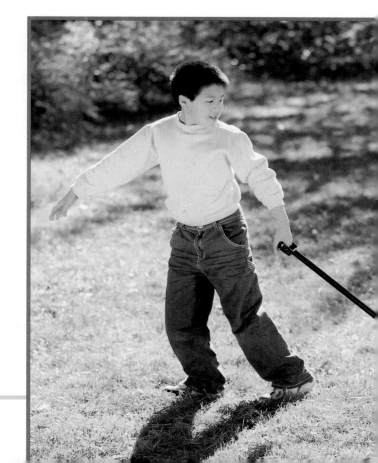

It takes less force to move something a short distance than a long distance. To move a ball a short distance, you kick it gently. To move it farther, you kick it hard.

■ **In which picture will the ball go farther? Why?**

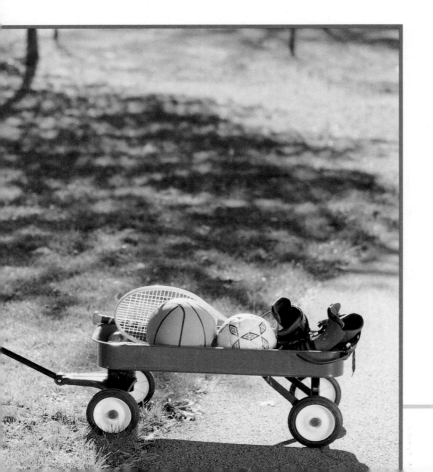

Ways to Measure Motion

You can measure how far an object or a person moves. In a jumping contest, you try to jump as far as you can. Someone measures how far you jump.

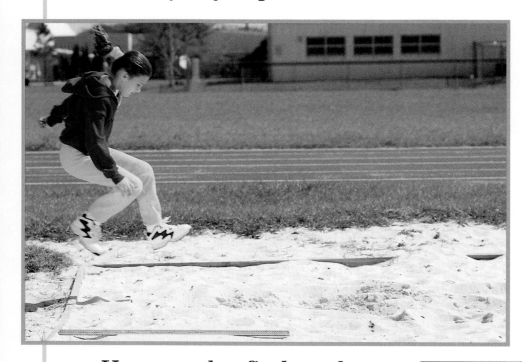

■ **What tool is being used to measure how far the girl jumps?**

You can also find out how fast or slowly someone or something moves. You measure the speed, or how much time the person or the object takes to move a certain distance. In a race, a timekeeper measures how much time racers take to reach the finish line.

02:47

You can use a rubber band to measure how much force it takes to move something. The rubber band stretches less when you pull with less force. It stretches more when you pull with more force.

- **Which picture shows more force being used?**

Think About It

1. What makes things move?

2. How can you measure motion?

Math/Literature Link

The Enormous Turnip

The folktale *The Enormous Turnip* is about a turnip so big that a man cannot pull it up. How will the man and his family pull up the turnip? You can read the book to find out how much force it takes.

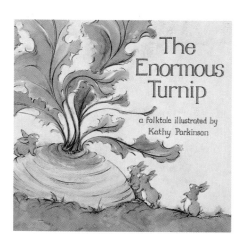

The Enormous Turnip

a folktale illustrated by Kathy Parkinson

Think and Do

See how much force it takes to move things. Tie a book to a spring scale. Pull on the spring scale. As the book moves, read the numbers on the scale. Repeat with other objects, and compare the numbers. Which object needs the most force to be moved?

Health Link

A Personal Trainer

A personal trainer teaches people how to exercise the right way. This personal trainer is showing a woman how to use a weight machine. The bar of this machine connects to weights. The woman must pull down on the bar to move the weights.

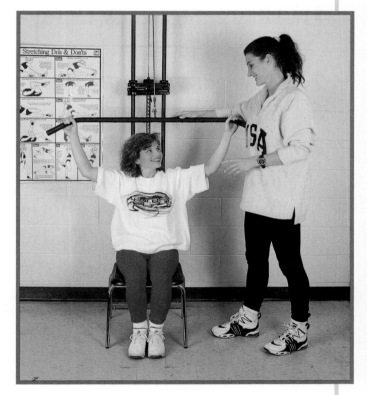

Write

Think of some exercises you know how to do. As you do each one, observe when you are pushing or pulling. Then write sentences to tell classmates how to do the exercises. Use the words *push* and *pull.*

Tell What You Know

Tell which picture answers each question.

1. How can gravity change an object's location?

2. How can you measure how far a thing moves?

3. How can you measure how long someone takes to move from one place to another?

4. Which is being moved by wind?

5. How can a push change an object's direction?

6. Which is a pull?

a.

b.

c.

d.

e.

f.

Vocabulary

7. Tell about the picture.

force   gravity   motion

Using Science Skills

8. **Observe** Make a chart like this one, and then observe objects in motion. Was it a push or a pull? Write whether a *push* or a *pull* moves each object.

Which Forces Move Objects?					
Object	Wind	Water	Gravity	Magnet	Other
Boat	push	push			

9. **Use Numbers** Make a ramp like this one. Place a toy car at the top, and let it go. Measure how far the car travels. Then cover the ramp with a thick towel and try again. When does the car travel farther? faster?

Try two other surfaces. Use numbers to measure each distance, and compare.

Hearing Sound

Vocabulary

sound
vibrate
loudness
pitch
sonar
music

Did You Know?

Elephants can make and hear sounds that are so low in **pitch** that humans can't hear them.

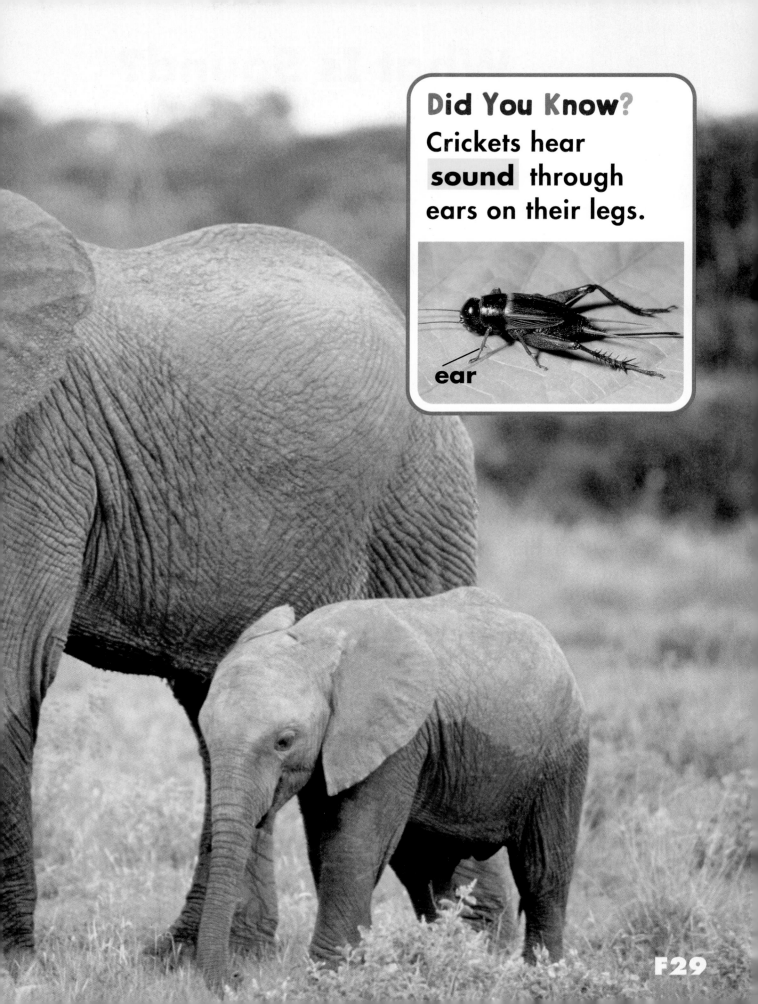

Did You Know?
Crickets hear **sound** through ears on their legs.

ear

What Is Sound?

What Makes Sound

You will need

ruler   paper and pencil

1 Hold the ruler on a desk so one end hangs over the edge. Push that end down and let it go.

2 Observe and record what happens.

3 How could you change the sound? Plan an investigation.

4 Follow your plan. Tell a classmate what you find out.

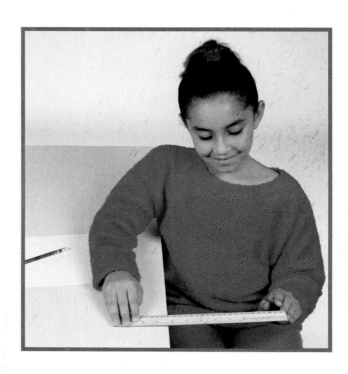

Science Skill
When you plan an investigation, you ask a question and test ways to answer the question.

What Makes Sound

The energy that you can hear is **sound**. Sound is made when things **vibrate**, or move back and forth, very fast.

Sound and Air

When something vibrates, it makes the air around it vibrate, too. The strings of a guitar vibrate when you pluck them. The vibrations travel through the air to your ears. Then you hear the sound the guitar makes.

Sound moves through the air in every direction. When a school bell rings, people all around the bell can hear it.

Sound can also be blocked. Some people who work near loud machines wear ear coverings. The coverings block some of the sound vibrations from reaching their ears.

■ **Why did this person cover his ears?**

How You Hear Sounds

You hear sounds with your ears. Sound vibrations move through the air into each ear. The vibrations reach your eardrum and make it vibrate.

eardrum

How You Make Sounds

You use your vocal cords to make sounds in your throat. Put your hand on your throat when you talk, and you can feel the vocal cords vibrate.

Audiologist

An audiologist tests people's hearing with machines that make sounds. An audiologist also helps people who do not hear well. You should get your hearing checked by an audiologist from time to time.

- **What is this audiologist doing?**

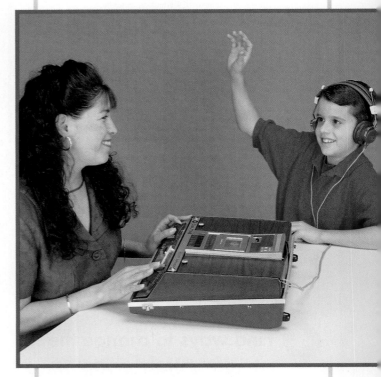

Think About It

1. What makes sound?
2. How do you hear sounds?

How Do Sounds Vary?

Investigate

Different Sounds

You will need

3 glasses

water

spoon

paper and pencil

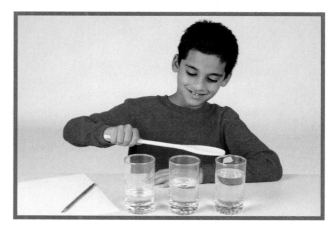

1️⃣ Pour a different amount of water into each glass.

2️⃣ Tap the side of each glass with the spoon.

3️⃣ Listen to the sounds. Record what you observe.

4️⃣ Find ways to change the sounds. Observe and record.

Science Skill
Listening is one way to observe.

How Sounds Can Be Different

Sounds are all around you. What sounds do you think the children in the picture hear? What sounds can you hear in your classroom?

Loud and Soft

Sounds are different in **loudness** , or how loud or soft they are. Some sounds, like yells, are loud. Other sounds, like whispers, are soft. It takes less energy to make a soft sound than a loud sound.

■ **What do you do to make a loud sound?**

High and Low

Sounds are also different in **pitch**, or how high or low they are. A sparrow's song is a high sound. A bullfrog's croak is a low sound.

■ How are the sounds a sparrow and a bullfrog make different?

Think About It

1. What are some loud sounds and some soft sounds?
2. What are some high sounds and some low sounds?

How Does Sound Travel?

How Sound Travels

You will need

meterstick

tape

paper and pencil

1 Measure 50 centimeters on your desk. Mark each end with tape.

2 Scratch one tape mark, and listen at the other end. Record what you hear.

3 Predict the loudness of the sound if you put your ear on the desk. Record what you predict.

4 Try it. What do you observe? Did you predict correctly?

Science Skill
To predict, think about what you already know and then say what you think will happen.

How Sound Travels

Sound can travel through different kinds of matter. These children have their ears under water. They can still hear the coach's voice. What kinds of matter are the sounds traveling through?

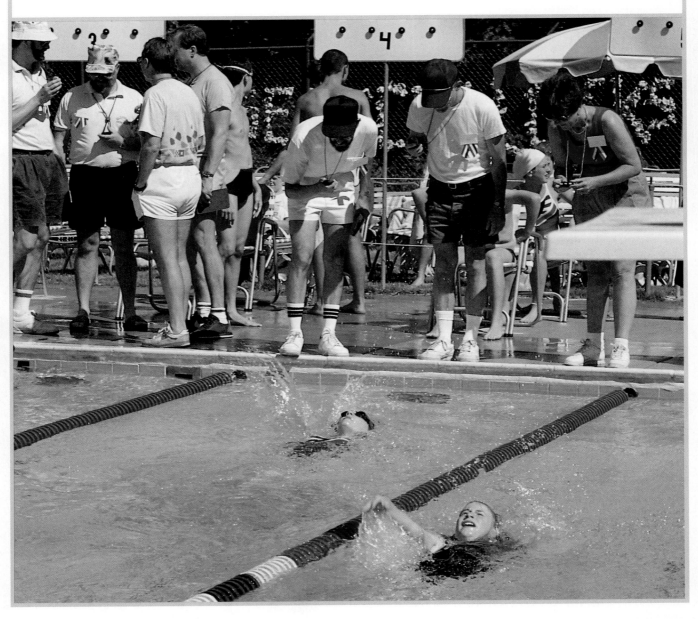

Sounds Travel Through Gases and Solids

Sounds can travel through gases such as air. The sound from the vibrating bells on some alarm clocks travels through the air. It reaches a person's ears and wakes the person up.

■ **What does the sound from the horn travel through?**

Sounds can also travel through solid objects. You may have played with a string telephone. A person talks into one cup, making the air inside it vibrate. The air makes the cup vibrate, and the cup makes the string vibrate.

The vibrations travel through the string and make the other cup vibrate. That cup makes the air inside it vibrate. The vibrations travel into the other person's ear, and that person hears the sound.

■ **What vibrates when a person talks into the cup?**

Sound Travels Through Liquids

Sounds can travel through liquids, such as water. Dolphins have a kind of **sonar**, or a way to use sounds to locate objects under water. The sounds make echoes when they hit objects. The dolphins locate the objects by listening to the echoes.

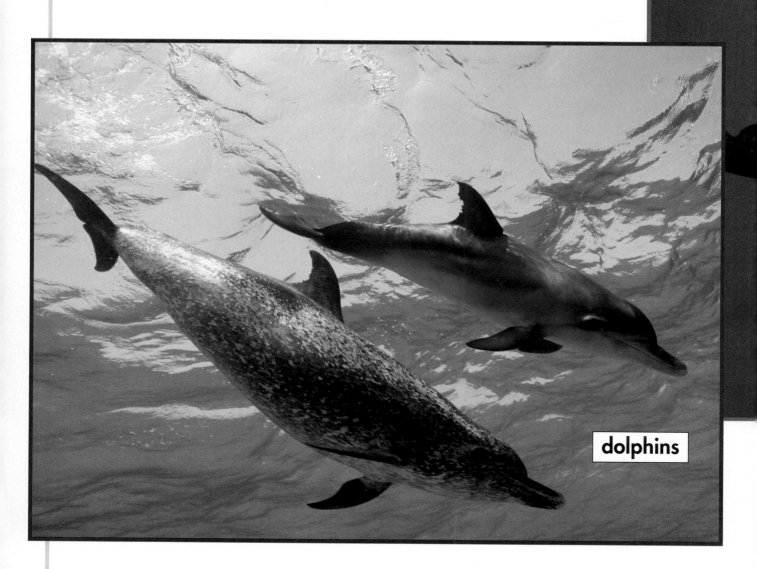

dolphins

Humpback whales also make sounds under water. The sounds they make are like songs. The songs can travel a long way through the water to other whales.

■ **What do you think this whale is communicating to her young?**

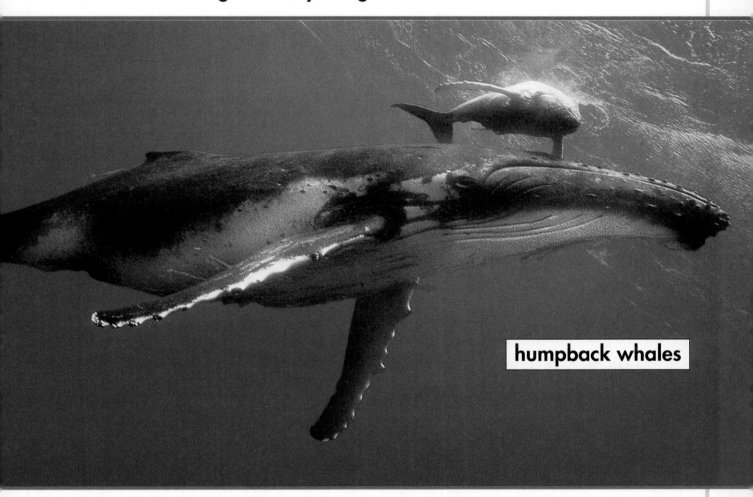

humpback whales

Think About It

1. How do sounds travel?
2. What can sounds travel through?

How Can We Make Different Sounds?

 Investigate

Making Different Sounds

You will need

rubber bands

box lid

pencil

1 Stretch 3 rubber bands around the box lid.

2 Pluck the rubber bands. Compare the sounds.

3 Put the pencil under the rubber bands and pluck them again. Compare.

4 How did the sounds change? How did they stay the same?

Science Skill
When you compare, you look for ways that two or more things are alike and different.

How to Make Different Sounds

People use sounds to make **music**, or a combination of sounds that people enjoy. These people are playing different musical instruments. Each instrument makes a different kind of sound.

Making Different Sounds

Some musical instruments have strings. Thin strings vibrate faster and make higher sounds. Thick strings vibrate more slowly and make lower sounds.

Changing the length of a string changes how fast it vibrates. Shortening a string makes it vibrate faster and sound higher. Making the string longer makes it vibrate more slowly and sound lower.

You can change the loudness of a sound. If you use a lot of energy and hit a drum hard, it makes a loud sound. If you use just a little energy and tap the drum lightly, it makes a soft sound.

■ **How can you make different sounds with these instruments?**

Think About It

1. How can you make high sounds and low sounds?
2. How can you make loud sounds and soft sounds?

Math Link

How Long Does a Sound Last?

This musical instrument is called a triangle. When a player taps the triangle, it makes a ringing sound.

Think and Do

Tap a triangle gently. Count slowly to time how long you can hear the sound. Then hit the triangle harder. Count at the same speed to time how long you can hear this sound.

Which sound lasts longer? Write a subtraction problem to show how much longer it lasted.

Music Link

Make Musical Instruments

Musical instruments can be grouped by the way they make sounds. Percussion instruments make sounds when you shake or hit them. Stringed instruments make sounds when you pluck their strings. Wind instruments make sounds when you blow into them.

percussion

stringed

wind

Write

Make a musical instrument of your own. Then draw or write about how it works. Tell if it is a wind, a stringed, or a percussion instrument.

Tell What You Know

Answer the question about each picture.

1. What vibrates to make the sound?

2. How can you change this sound?

3. How are these sounds different?

Vocabulary

Use each word to tell about a picture.

4. sonar

5. music

6. pitch

a.

b.

c.

Using Science Skills

7. Observe/Compare Make a chart like this one. Then listen for different sounds. Write the information in your chart.

Kinds of Sounds		
Sound Maker	High or Low	Loud or Soft

8. Plan an Investigation/Compare Investigate how to change the pitch of a sound. Blow into an empty bottle. Listen to the sound. Now think of ways to change its pitch. Try out your ideas.

Push or Pull Toys?

1. Observe some toys. Do you push them or pull them or both?

2. Make a chart to classify the toys as toys you push, toys you pull, or both.

3. Use your chart to help you communicate to classmates what you observe.

Magnetic Puppet Show

1. Draw puppets on cardboard. Cut them out.

2. Bend the bottom of the puppet back to make a tab. Tape a paper clip onto the tab.

3. Cut off one side of a box to make a stage.

4. Place the puppets on the stage.

5. Use magnets under the stage to move the puppets around.

Make Chicken Sounds

1. Punch two holes in the bottom of a paper cup.

2. Push a string through the holes and tie a knot.

3. Wet the string. Move your fingers along the string in short, jerky movements.

4. Tell what sounds you hear and how they are made.

Play a Listening Game

1. All players but the one who is "it" close their eyes.

2. The player who is "it" makes a sound.

3. The other players guess how the sound is being made. They may need clues from the player who is "it."

4. The first player to guess correctly makes the next sound.

Museum of Science and Industry, Chicago, Illinois

At this museum, you can learn about forces and motion. You can see how forces make a plane fly. You can also see other exhibits that show how forces and motion are used.

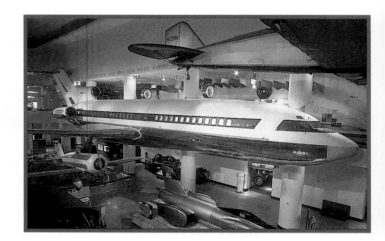

Plan Your Own Expedition

Visit an exhibit or a museum near you. Or log on to The Learning Site.

GO ONLINE www.harcourtschool.com

References

Science Handbook

Using Science Tools

Hand Lens

A hand lens makes things look larger than they are.

1. Hold the hand lens close to your face.
2. Move the object until you see it clearly.

Thermometer

Scientists use the Celsius scale on a thermometer to measure temperature.

1. Place the thermometer in the liquid.
2. Wait about two minutes.
3. Find the line that meets the top of the liquid.
4. Read the number. This is the temperature.

The temperature is 40°C.

This leaf is 21 centimeters long.

Ruler

A ruler is a tool that lets you measure how long something is.

1. Put the edge of the ruler at the end of the object.
2. Read the number at the other end.

Meterstick

A meterstick is a tool that lets you measure in centimeters.

1. Put the beginning edge of the meterstick at the beginning point.
2. Read the number at the other end to measure the distance.

This paper is 30 centimeters long.

Measuring Cup

Use a measuring cup to measure how much liquid there is.

1. Pour the liquid into the cup.
2. Put the cup on a table.
3. Wait until the liquid is still.
4. Look at the level of the liquid.
5. Read how much liquid is in the cup.

There are 350 milliliters of liquid here.

Clock

A clock lets you measure time. Some clocks have a minute hand and an hour hand.

1. Look at the hour hand.
2. Look at the minute hand.
3. Read the time.

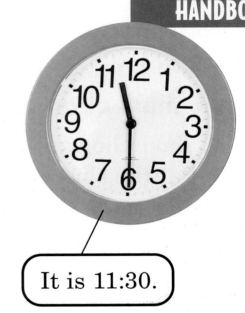

It is 11:30.

Stopwatch

A stopwatch measures how much time passes.

1. To start timing, press START.
2. To stop timing, press STOP.
3. Read how much time has passed.

Twenty-five seconds have gone by.

Balance

Use a balance to measure the mass of an object.

1. Make the pans even.
2. Put the object in one pan.
3. Add masses to the other pan until the pans are even again.
4. Count up the number of masses. The total is the mass of the object.

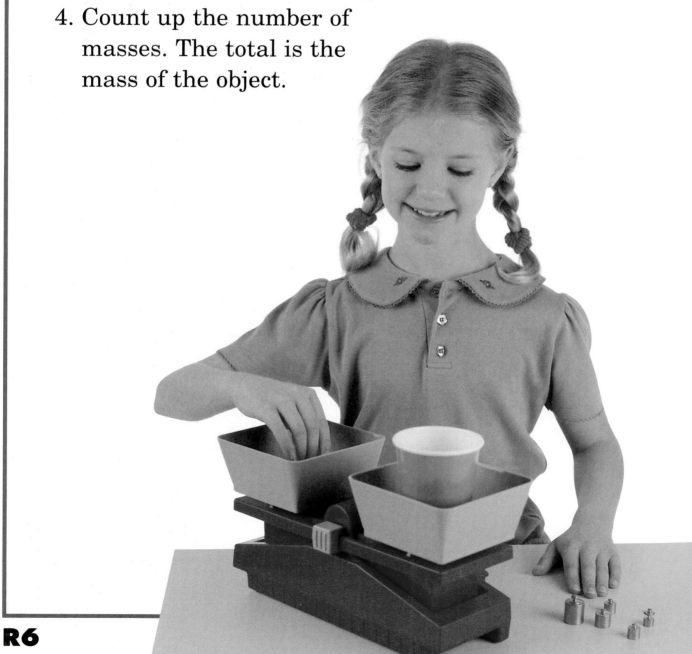

Magnet

Use a magnet to attract things made of iron or steel.

1. Place one of the magnet's poles near the object.
2. See if the magnet attracts the object.
3. Do not drop or hit the magnet.
4. Do not put the magnet near a computer or other objects that have a magnet inside.
5. When you store the magnet, attach another magnet or a piece of steel to the poles.

Measurements

1 cm

centimeter (cm) ruler

1 in.

inch (in.) ruler

Water freezes at 32°F.

Fahrenheit (F) temperature

Water freezes at 0°C.

Celsius (C) temperature

1 kilogram (kg)

1 pound (lb)

1 liter (L)

1 cup (c)

Health Handbook

Getting Exercise

Warm-Up and Cool-Down Stretches

▼ **Shoulder and Chest Stretch** Pull your hands slowly toward the floor. Keep your elbows straight, but don't lock them.

Warm up your muscles before you exercise. Spend at least five minutes stretching. You can use any of the stretches shown here. Hold each stretch while you count to 15. Repeat each stretch three times. Remember to start exercising slowly.

Slow down at the end of exercise. Then repeat some of these stretches for about two minutes. Stretching after exercise helps your muscles cool down.

▶ **Sit-and-Reach Stretch** Bend forward at the waist. Keep watching your toes.

◀ **Calf Stretch** Keep both feet on the floor. Try changing the distance between your feet. Where do you get a better stretch?

▲ **Upper Back and Shoulder Stretch**
Try to stretch your hand down so
that it rests flat against your back.

▼ **Thigh Stretch** Keep both hands
flat on the ground. Lean as far
forward as you can.

▲ **Leg Stretch**
Extend one leg
behind you. Keep
the toes of that
foot pointed up.

Tips for Stretching

- Never bounce. Stretch gently.
- Breathe normally to get the air you need.
- Never stretch until it hurts. You should
  feel only a slight pull.

Getting Exercise

Build Your Heart and Lungs

Exercise helps your heart and lungs grow strong. The best exercise activities make you breathe deeply. They make your heart beat fast. You should try to exercise for at least twenty minutes at a time. Remember to warm up first and cool down at the end.

▲ **Swimming** If you are not a strong swimmer, use a kickboard to get a good workout. Remember to swim only when a lifeguard is present.

◄ **Skating** Always wear a helmet, elbow and knee pads, wrist guards, and gloves. Learn to skate, stop, and fall correctly.

▼ **Riding a Bike** When you ride your bike, your exercise really gets you somewhere! Follow bike safety rules, and always wear your helmet.

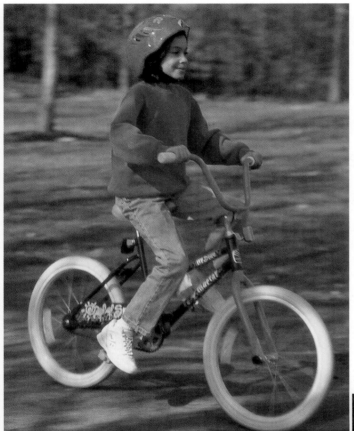

► **Walking** A fast walk can help build your heart and lungs. Wear shoes that support your feet. Walk with a friend for extra fun!

► **Jumping Rope** Jumping rope is good for your heart and your lungs. Always jump on a flat surface. Wear shoes that support your feet.

R13

Staying Safe

Fire Safety

You can stay safe from fires. Follow these safety rules.

- Never play with matches or lighters.
- Be careful around stoves, heaters, fireplaces, and grills.
- Don't use microwaves, irons, or toasters without an adult's help.
- Practice your family's fire safety plan.
- If there is a fire in your home, get out quickly. Drop to the floor and crawl if the room is filled with smoke. If a closed door feels hot, don't open it. Use another exit. Call 911 from outside your home.
- If your clothes catch on fire, use Stop, Drop, and Roll right away to put out the flames.

❶ **Stop.** Don't run or wave your arms.

❷ **Drop.** Lie down quickly. Cover your eyes with your hands.

❸ **Roll.** Roll back and forth to put out the fire.

Stranger Danger

You can stay safe around strangers. Follow these rules.

- Never talk to strangers.
- Never go with a stranger, on foot or in a car.
- If you are home alone, do not open the door. Do not let telephone callers know you are alone.
- Never give your name, address, or phone number to anyone you don't know. (You may give this information to a 911 operator in an emergency.)
- If you are lost or need help, talk to a police officer, a guard, or a store clerk.
- If a stranger bothers you, use the Stranger Danger rules to stay safe.

❶ **Say no!** Yell if you need to. You do not have to be polite to strangers.

❷ **Get away.** Walk fast or run in the opposite direction. Go toward people who can help you.

❸ **Tell someone.** Tell a trusted adult, such as a family member, a teacher, or a police officer. Do not keep secrets about strangers.

Bike Safety

A Safe Bike

To ride your bike safely, you need to start with a safe bike. A safe bike is the right size for you. When you sit on your bike with the pedal in the lowest position, you should be able to rest your heel on the pedal.

After checking the size of your bike, check to see that it has the right safety equipment. Your bike should have everything shown below.

horn

white reflector

red reflector

clear reflector

clear reflector

reflectors

Your Bike Helmet

◀ Always wear a bike helmet. Wear your helmet flat on your head. Be sure it is strapped tightly. If your helmet gets bumped in a fall, replace it right away, even if it doesn't look damaged.

Safety on the Road

- Check your bike for safety every time you ride it.
- Ride in single file. Ride in the same direction as traffic.
- Stop, look, listen, and think when you enter a street or cross a driveway.
- Walk your bike across an intersection.
- Obey all traffic signs and signals.
- Don't ride at night without an adult. Wear light-colored clothing and use lights and reflectors for night riding.

Sense Organs

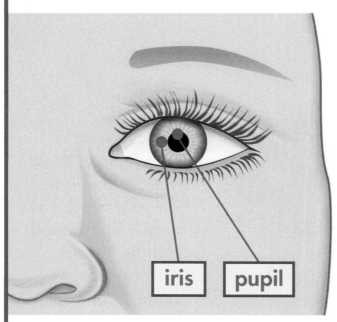

Outside of Eye

Caring for Your Eyes and Ears

- Sunglasses protect your eyes. Wear sunglasses when you are outdoors in sunlight or snow or on the water.
- Never put anything in your ears.

Eyes

Your eyes let you see. When you look at your eyes, you see a white part, a colored part, and a hole. The colored part is the iris. The hole in the middle is the pupil.

Inside of Eye

inner ear middle ear outer ear

Inside of Ear   **Outside of Ear**

Ears

Your ears let you hear. What you see on the outside of your head is only part of your ear. The main part of your ear is inside your head.

ACTIVITIES

1. Put your hand over one eye for thirty seconds. Look in a mirror and take your hand away from your eye. What happens to the pupil of that eye?

2. Put on a blindfold and cover one ear. Ask a classmate to stand somewhere in the room and clap. Point to where the sound came from. Are you pointing in the right direction?

The Respiratory System

When you breathe, you are using your respiratory system. Your mouth, your nose, your lungs, and your diaphragm are parts of your respiratory system.

Caring for Your Respiratory System

- Never put anything in your nose.
- Playing helps your lungs. When you climb and jump, you breathe harder. Breathing harder makes your lungs stronger.

nose

mouth

lungs

Mouth and Nose

Air goes in and out of your body through your mouth and nose. Your mouth and nose warm the air you breathe.

Lungs

You have two lungs. Your lungs are in your chest. When you breathe in, your lungs fill with air. When you breathe out, air leaves your lungs.

ACTIVITIES

1. Try to say something while you're breathing in. Try to say something while you're breathing out. Which is easier?

2. Breathe onto a mirror. What happens? Rinse your mouth with cold water. Again breathe on the mirror. What happens?

The Muscular System

The muscles in your body help you move. When you blink, you are using muscles. When you run, you are using muscles. Even when you eat, you are using muscles.

Caring for Your Muscular System

Stretch your muscles before you use them for play or exercise.

ACTIVITY

Wiggle your nose. Stick out your tongue. Wrinkle your forehead. Smile. Are you using muscles?

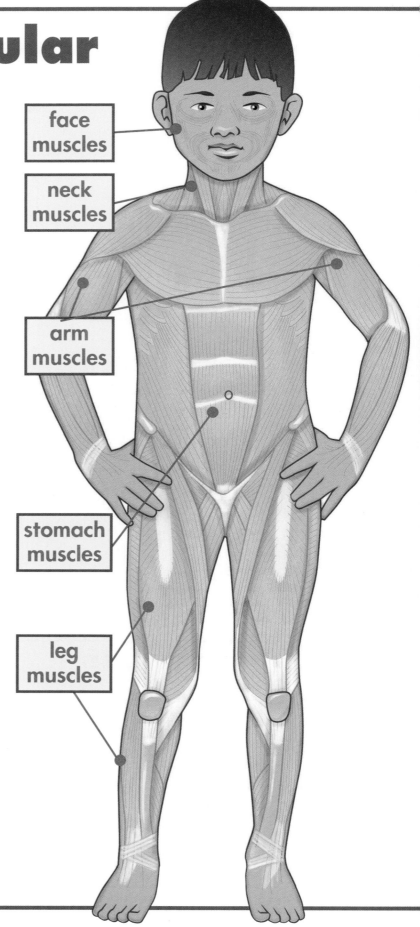

face muscles

neck muscles

arm muscles

stomach muscles

leg muscles

The Nervous System

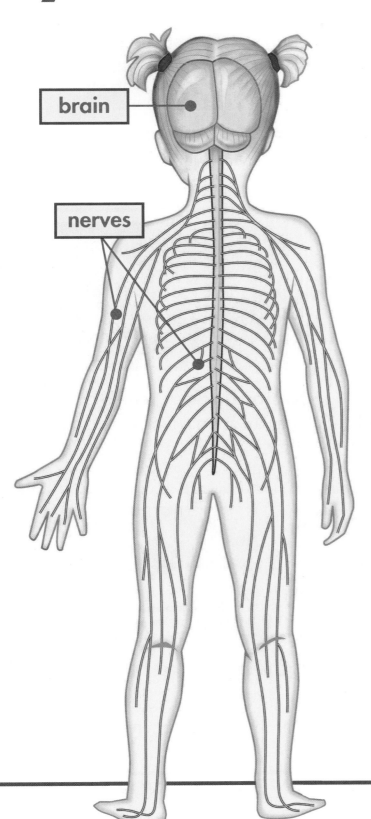

brain

nerves

Your nervous system makes your muscles work and tells you about your surroundings. Your brain and your nerves are parts of your nervous system.

Caring for Your Nervous System

Get plenty of sleep. Sleeping lets your brain rest.

ACTIVITY

Have a classmate blindfold you and fill one cup with cold water and another cup with warm water. Stick your finger in each cup. Can you tell which is the cold water and which is the warm water?

GLOSSARY

A

adaptation [ad′ap•ta′shən] Anything about an animal that helps it live. The way a chameleon changes color is an adaptation. (B21)

amphibian [am•fib′ē•ən] An animal that lives both in water and on land. A frog is an amphibian. (A27)

B

blizzard [bliz′ərd] A storm with heavy snow and strong winds. (D57)

C

cactus [kak′təs] A plant that can store water in its thick stems. A cactus grows in the desert. (A17)

camouflage [kam′ə•flazh′] A way an animal looks that helps it hide. Coloring is one kind of camouflage. (B22)

centimeter [sen′tə•mēt′ər] A unit used to measure length. A crayon is about 9 centimeters long. (E13)

R24

cirrus [sir′əs] A kind of cloud that is thin, feathery, and high in the sky. We see cirrus clouds in sunny weather. (D50)

cumulus [kyōom′yə•ləs] A kind of cloud that looks like puffy white cotton. We see cumulus clouds in fair weather. (D51)

constellation
[kon′stə•lā′shən]
A group of stars that form a star picture. Orion is a constellation. (D8)

D

desert [dez′ərt] An environment that gets little rain. Only a few kinds of plants and animals live in the desert. (B10)

crater [krā′tər] A hole that has the shape of a bowl. The moon has craters. (D26)

digest
[di•jest′] To break down food in the body. It is harder to digest an apple than apple juice. (A61)

R25

dinosaur [dī′nə·sôr′] An animal that lived millions of years ago. Tyrannosaurus rex was a dinosaur. (C37)

energy [en′ər·jē] Something that can cause change and do work. Light and heat are kinds of energy. (D14)

drought [drout] A long time without rain. Many plants die during a drought. (B42)

environment [in•vī′rən•mənt] All the living and nonliving things in a place. A forest is a land environment. (B5)

endangered [in•dān′jərd] In danger of not being alive any more. Sea turtles are endangered animals. (B51)

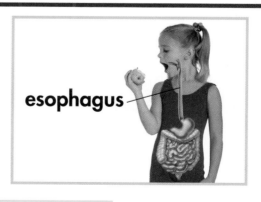

esophagus

esophagus [i•sof′ə•gəs] The tube that goes from your mouth to your stomach. (A62)

estivate [es′tə•vāt′] To stay in a deep sleep during the summer. Some toads estivate to escape the hot, dry summer. (B27)

food chain [food′ chān′] The order in which animals eat plants and other animals. (B32)

evaporate [i•vap′ə•rāt′] To change into a gas. Water in a puddle will evaporate in the warm sun. (D44)

force [fôrs] A push or a pull that makes something move. Magnetism is one kind of force. (F5)

extinct [ik•stingkt′] No longer living. Because dinosaurs do not live anymore, they are extinct. (C34)

forest [fôr′ist] An environment that gets enough rain and warmth for many trees to grow. (B12)

fossil [fos′əl] What is left of a plant or an animal that lived long ago. A fossil can be a print of an animal's bones. (C25)

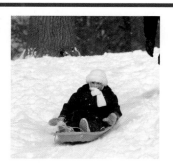

gravity [grav′ə•tē] A force that pulls things toward the center of Earth. A sled moves down a hill because of gravity. (F11)

gas [gas] The only kind of matter that always fills all the space inside a container. Balloons are filled with a gas. (E21)

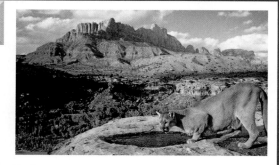

habitat [hab′ə•tat′] A place where an animal finds the things it needs to live. In its habitat this animal finds water. (B6)

germinate [jûr′mə•nāt′] To start to grow. A seed may germinate if it gets water and warmth. (A10)

heart [härt] A muscle that pumps blood to every part of the body. Your heart is the size of your fist. (A55)

heart rate

[härt rāt] The number of times a heart beats each minute. Exercise makes a heart rate faster. (A56)

I

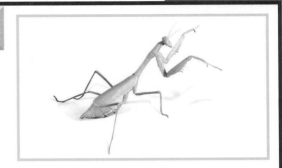

insect

[in′sekt′] An animal that has three body parts and six legs. Ants and bees are each a kind of insect. (A28)

hibernate

[hī′bər•nāt′] To spend the winter in a deep sleep. Some hedgehogs hibernate in winter. (B26)

irreversible

[ir′i•vûr′sə•bəl] Not able to be changed back. Cooking an egg causes an irreversible change. (E48)

hurricane

[hûr′ə•kān′] A very large storm with strong winds, high ocean waves, and heavy rain. (D57)

L

life cycle

[līf′ sī′kəl] All the parts of an animal's life from birth to death. The life cycle of a bird has different stages. (A31)

R29

liquid [lik′wid] A form of matter that does not have its own shape. Water, milk, juice, and gasoline are each a liquid. (E15)

loudness [loud′nis] A measure of how loud or soft a sound is. Loudness depends on the amount of energy used to make the sound. (F38)

litter [lit′ər] Trash that is not put in a trash can. Plants and animals are hurt by litter. (B48)

lungs [lungz] Body parts that help you breathe the air you need to live. When you breathe in, air moves into your lungs. (A55)

living [liv′ing] Growing and changing. Plants and animals are living things because they need food, water, and air. (A5)

M

magnet [mag′nit] A piece of iron or steel that attracts, or pulls, iron and steel. (F13)

mammal [mam'əl] An animal that has fur or hair. A mother mammal makes milk to feed to her young. A cat is a mammal. (A26)

medicine [med'ə•sən] A product that helps people when they are sick or hurt. Many medicines are made from plants. (C13)

mass [mas] The amount of matter an object has. You can use a balance to see how much mass an object has. (E7)

migrate [mī'grāt'] To move as a group to live in another place. Some ducks migrate in winter. (B24)

matter [mat'ər] The material that all things are made of. People, clothing, air, and water are all made of matter. (E5)

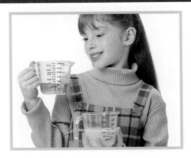

milliliter [mil'ə•lē'tər] A unit used to measure the volume of a liquid. Some measuring cups measure in milliliters. (E19)

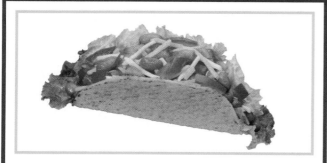

mixture [miks′chər] Two or more things that have been mixed together without being changed. Taco filling is a mixture. (E36)

motion [mō′shən] The act of moving. People, animals, and things are in motion when they move. (F19)

moon [mōon] The object that appears the largest in the night sky. The moon takes about one month to orbit Earth. (D25)

muscles [mus′əlz] Body parts that move your bones and do other jobs. Your muscles work in pairs. (A51)

moonlight [mōon′līt′] The light from the moon. Light from the sun that bounces off the moon is called moonlight. (D25)

music [myōo′zik] A combination of sounds that people enjoy. You can use an instrument to make music. (F47)

N

natural resource

[nach′ər•əl rē′sôrs′]
Something found in nature that people can use to meet their needs. Plants are one natural resource. (C6)

O

orbit   [ôr′bit] The path around
something. Earth's orbit around the sun takes one year. (D20)

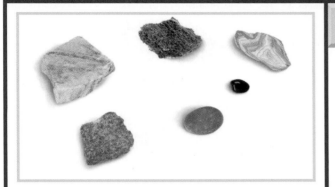

nonliving   [non•liv′ing] Not
alive. Air, water, and rocks are non-living things. (A5)

P

paleontologist
[pā′lē•on•tol′ə•jist] A scientist who finds and studies fossils. Some pale-ontologists study dinosaurs. (C27)

nutrients   [nōō′trē•ənts] Min-
erals. Plants need nutrients from the soil to grow. (A9)

permanent teeth
[pûr′mə•nənt tēth] New adult teeth that take the place of first teeth. People have 32 permanent teeth. (A46)

pitch [pich] A measure of how high or low a sound is. The pitch of a cat's meow is higher than the pitch of a lion's roar. (F39)

pond [pond] A freshwater environment. Otters, turtles, and frogs live around a pond. (B15)

planet [plan′it] A large ball of rock or gas that moves around the sun. Earth is our planet. (D10)

property [prop′ər•tē] A quality of something. Color, size, shape, and texture are each a property. (E7)

pollution [pə•loo′shən] Waste that harms land, water, or air. Factories, farms, and cars can make pollution. (B47)

R

rain forest [rān′fôr′ist] An environment where rain falls almost every day. Many kinds of plants live in a rain forest. (B11)

reconstruct [rē′kən•strukt′] To rebuild. Scientists try to reconstruct dinosaur skeletons. (C32)

resource [rē′sôrs′] Anything that people can use. People use resources for food and shelter. (C6)

recycle [rē•sī′kəl] To use old materials to make new things. You can recycle metal, plastic, and paper to make other things. (B55)

reuse [rē′yōōz′] To use again. You can reuse a water bottle as a vase. (B55)

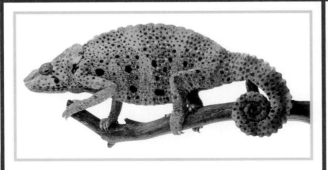

reptile [rep′tīl] An animal that has scales and rough, dry skin. Snakes and lizards are each a kind of reptile. (A27)

reversible [ri•vûr′sə•bəl] Able to be changed. The freezing of water to form ice is a reversible change. (E43)

rock [rok] A hard, nonliving thing that comes from the Earth. People use rocks to build roads and buildings. (C5)

season [sē′zən] A time of the year. The four seasons are spring, summer, fall, and winter. (D20)

rotation [rō•tā′shən] The spinning of Earth. One complete rotation of Earth takes about 24 hours. (D16)

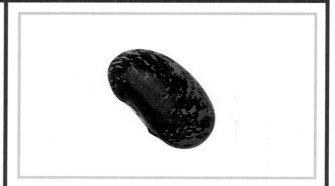

seed coat [sēd′ kōt] A covering that protects a seed. The seed coat is one part of a seed. (A10)

saliva [sə•lī′və] The liquid in your mouth that begins to break down food. Food mixes with saliva when you chew. (A62)

seedling [sēd′ling] A young plant. A seedling grows and changes. (A10)

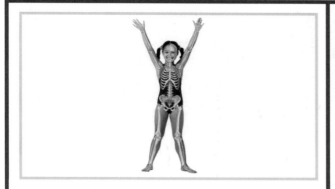

skeleton [skel′ə•tən] The bones of the body that hold it up and give it shape. (A50)

solar system [sō′lər sis′təm] The sun and its nine planets. In the solar system, the planets move around the sun. (D10)

soil [soil] The loose top layer of the Earth's surface. People use soil to grow food. (C5)

solid [sol′id] The only form of matter that has a shape of its own. Books, furniture, and cars are each a solid. (E9)

solar energy [sō′lər en′ər•jē] Light and heat from the sun. Living things on Earth are warmed by solar energy. (D15)

sonar [sō′när′] A way to use sounds to locate objects underwater. Dolphins use a natural sonar by listening to echoes. (F44)

sound [sound] Energy that you hear. A sound can be loud or soft. (F31)

stratus [strat′əs] A kind of cloud that is low and gray and stretches across the sky. Stratus clouds can bring rain. (D50)

star [stär] A large ball of hot gases. The sun is the star closest to Earth. (D6)

sun [sun] The star closest to Earth. The sun is much larger than it looks from Earth. (D10)

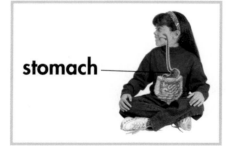

stomach

stomach [stum′ək] A body part made of muscles that squeeze food and mix it with special juices. (A63)

T

temperature [tem′pər•ə•chər] A measure of how hot or cold something is. In summer the temperature of the air is higher than in winter. (D48)

60°

thermometer

[thər•mom′ə•tər] A tool that measures temperature. You can use a thermometer to measure air temperature. (D48)

transportation

[trans′pər•tā′shən] Ways to move people or things. Ships, cars, and airplanes are kinds of transportation. (C17)

thunderstorm

[thun′dər•stôrm′] A storm with rain, thunder, and lightning. (D56)

Triceratops [trī•ser′ə•tops′] A kind of dinosaur that had three horns on its head. Triceratops was a plant eater. (C38)

tornado

[tôr•nā′dō] A funnel-shaped, spinning cloud with strong winds. A tornado can destroy buildings. (D56)

tundra [tun′drə] A place with a cold and windy environment with no trees. The land is covered with ice and snow for most of the year. (B13)

vibrate [vī′brāt′] To move back and forth. The strings of a guitar vibrate when you pluck them. (F31)

weather [weth′ər] The way the air is outside. The weather is often sunny and hot in summer. (D37)

water cycle [wô′tər sī′kəl] The movement of water from the air to the land and back to the air. (D43)

wind [wind] Moving air. Wind can move kites, pinwheels, and wind vanes. (F10)

water vapor [wô′tər vā′pər] Water that has changed into a gas. When water is heated enough, it becomes water vapor. (D44)

Photography Credits

Page Placement Key: (t) top, (b) bottom, (c) center, (l) left, (r) right, (bg) background, (fg) foreground, (i) inset.

Cover and Title page: Corbis Images

Table of Contents: Pg *4 (fg) J &W Waldman/Bruce Coleman, Inc.; (bg) Keith Lanpher/Liaison International; *5 fg) Howard Grey/Stone; (bg) Alan Kearney/FPG International; *6 C1 Into The Wind; (bg) Simon Fraser/SPLPhoto Researchers.

Unit A: Pg A1 (fg) J &W Waldman/Bruce Coleman, Inc.; (bg) Keith Lanpher/Liaison International; A2-3 Ken Biggs/Stone; A3 (i) Connie Hansen/The Stock Market; A6 (b) Tim Davis/Photo Researchers, Inc.; A6 (t) John D. Cunningham/Visuals Unlimited; A11 (bi) Maxmilian Stock Ltd./Earth Scenes; A12 Grant Heilman Photography; A13 (b) David R. Frazier; A13 (t) Cathlyn Melloan/Stone; A15 (b) Morey K. Milbradt/Panoramic Images; A15 (c) Gary Irving/Panoramic Images; A15(t) Pete Winkel/Stock South/PictureQuest; A16 (b) Runk/Schoenberger/Grant Heilman Photography; A16 (c) Michael Groen Photography; A16 (cb) Superstock; A16 (c) Dr. Wm. M. Harlow/Photo Researchers; A16 (t) Doug Sokell/Tom Stack & Associates; A17 (c) Superstock; A17 (l) Gene Ahrens/Bruce Coleman Inc.; A17 (r) Doug Sokell/Tom Stack & Associates, A18 (b) C. I. Bernard/Animals Animals/Earth Scenes; Al 8 (c) J.C. Carton/Bruce Coleman; A18 (t) Danilo Donadoni/Bruce Coleman; A20 (c) E.R. Degginger/ Bruce Coleman; A20 (i) Jeff Foott/DRK Photo; A20 (r) Wayne Lankinen/DRK Photo; A21 Michael Groen Photography; A22-23 Flip Nicklin/Minden Pictures; A23 Richard R. Hansen/Photo Researchers, Inc.; A25 (b) John E. Swedberg/Bruce Coleman Inc.; A25 (cb) Mark Wagoner/Gamma-Liaison International; A25 (ct) Tom Veco/The Wildlife Collection; A25 (r) Peter Davey/Bruce Coleman Inc.; A25 (t) S. I. Krasemann/Photo Researchers, Inc.; A26 (b) Wayne Lankinen/DRK Photo; A26 (t) G. Robert Bishop/Stone; A27 (b) Denise Tackett/Tom Stack & Associates; A27 (c) Michael Fogden/DRK Photo; A27 (t) Renee Lynn/Stone; A28 (b) J. Carmichael/Bruce Cole-man Inc.; A28 (t) Marty Curdano/DRK Photo; A29 (l) Brian Parker/Tom Stack & Associates; A29 (r) Rex Ziak/Stone; A31 (b) S. J. Krasemann/Peter Arnold, Inc.; A31 (t) Mark Newman/Bruce Coleman Inc.; A32 (b) William H. Mullins/Photo Researchers, Inc.; A32 (t) Tim Davis/Photo Researchers, Inc.; A33 (b) Jennifer Loomis/Animals Animals/Earth Scenes; A33 (c) Michael Habicht/Animals Animals/Earth Scenes; A33 (t) Arthur C. Twomey/Photo Researchers, Inc.; A34 Jane Burton/Bruce Coleman Inc.; A34 (rc) Carolyn A. McKeone/Photo Researchers, Inc.; A35 (l) Jane Burton/AG Stock USA; A36 David M. Dennis/Tom Stack & Associates; A37 (c) Patricia Doyle/Stone; A37 (l) Renee Lynn/Stone; A37 (r) Breck P. Kent/Animals Animals/Earth Scenes; A37 (t) Lemoine Iacana/Photo Researchers, Inc., A38 Kathi Lamm/Stone; A39(l) Ed Reschke/Peter Arnold, Inc.; A39(cl) Rod Planck/Photo Researchers, Inc.; A39(cr) Jeff Foot/DRK Photo; A39(r) D. Cavagnaro/DRK Photo; A40-41 Index Stock Photography; A43(frames) Michael Groen Photography; A43(l) Mary T. Murphy; A43(r) Mary Kay Taylor; A44-45 Stephen Ogilvy/Picture It; A46 Paul Avis/Gamma-Liaison International; A47 (l) Steve Dunwell/Image Bank; A49-52(l) Stephen Ogilvy/Picture It; A52-53 David Madison/Bruce Coleman Inc.; A53 S. Villeger/Photo Researchers; A55-57 Stephen Ogilvy/Picture It; A59 Tom Dee Ann McCarthy/The Stock Market; A61-63 Stephen Ogilvy/Picture It; A64 Richard Hutchings/Picture It; A66 Mehan Kulyk/Science photo Library/Photo Researchers; A68 Stephen Ogilvy/Picture It; A72 Jackson Zoo.

Unit B: B1 (fg) Howard Grey/Stone; (bg) Alan Kearney/FPG International; B2-3 Frans Lanting/Minden Pictures; B5 Kim Heacox /DRK Photo; B6 (b) Stephen I. Krasemann/DRK Photo; B6 (c) Bill Bachmann/Stock, Boston,; B6 (l) Bill Beatty/Visuals Unlimited; B7 (b) Martin Harvey/The Wildlife Collection; B7 (c) Jeff Foott/Bruce Coleman Inc.; B7 (t) Ken W. Davis/Tom Stack & Associates; B9 (bl) Carr Cliffton/Minden Pictures; B9 (br) Wayne Lynch/DRK Photo; B9 (tl) Larry Ulrich/DRK Photo; B9 (tr) Doug Wechsler/Animals Animals/Earth Scenes; B10 (b) Joe McDonald/DRK Photo; B10 (c) Larry Ulrich/DRK Photo; B10 (t) Craig K. Lorenz/Photo Researchers, Inc.; B11 (b) Dr. Paul A. Zahl/Photo Researchers, Inc.; B11 (bg) Doug Wechsler/Animals Animals/Earth Scenes; B11 (c) N.H. Cheatham/DRK Photo; B11 (t) Joe McDonald/Animals Animals/Earth Scenes; B12 (b) Art Wolfe/Stone; B12 (c) S. Nielsen/DRK Photo; B12 (t) Carr Clifton/Minden Pictures; B13(l) Wayne Lynch/DRK Photo; B13(r) Johnny Johnson/Animals Animals/Earth Scenes; B15 (b) Valerie Hodgson/Visuals Unlimited; B15 (t) David Sieren/Visuals Unlimited; B16-B17 (b) Doug Sokell/Visuals Unlimited; B16 (c) Tom Brakefield/Bruce Coleman Inc.; B16 (t) Tim Fitzharris/Minden Pictures; B17 (t) Hans Pfletschinger/Peter Arnold, Inc.; B18(b) Flip Micklin/Minden Pictures; B18 (t)-19(l) M.C. Chamberlain/DRK Photo; B19 (c) Bruce Coleman Inc.; B19 (r) Flip Schulke/Black Star; B21 E.R. Degginger/Photo Researchers, Inc.; B22 (bl) David Hall/Photo Researchers, Inc.; B22 (tr) Dan Guravich/Photo Researchers, Inc.; B22-23 C. Clem Haagner/Photo Researchers, Inc.; B23 (t) M. K. Ranjitsinh/Photo Researchers, Inc.; B24 (l) Laurie Campbell; B24-25 (t) Kennan Ward/The Stock Market; B24-25 (b) Art Wolfe; B26 (bl) Jane Burton/Bruce Coleman Inc.; B26 (tr) Ken Highfill/Photo Researchers, Inc.; B26-B27 (b) Lynn Rogers/Peter Arnold, Inc.; B27(t) Jeff Lepore/Photo Researchers, Inc.; B29 Bruce Gaylord/Visuals Unlimited; B30(b)-B31(b) Paul Mozell/Stock, Boston; B30(c) Arthur Morris/Visuals Unlimited; B30(t) Franz Lanting/Minden Pictures; B31(t) Gregory K. Scott/Photo Researchers, Inc.; B34(c) S.L. Pimm/Visuals Unlimited; B34(t) Larry Ulrich/DRK Photo; B35(c) Tom Lewis; B36(bl) Doug Wechsler/Animals Animals, Earth Scenes; B36(br) Larry Ulrich/DRK Photo; B36(tc) Scott Nielsen/Bruce Coleman; B36(tl) David Sieren/Visuals Unlimited; B36(tr) Wayne Lynch/DRK Photo; B37 Stephen Ogilvy/Picture It; B39 Roy Morsch/The Stock Market; B41 John Eastcott/Yva Momatiuk/Stock, Boston; B42 Tom McHugh/Photo Researchers, Inc.; B43(l) Charlie Palek/Animals Animals/Earth Scenes; B43(r) Vince Streano/The Stock Market; B44 (b) John M. Roberts/The Stock Market; B44(t) Thomas Ives/The Stock Market; B45 (t) Jim Steinberg/Photo Researchers, Inc.; B47 Peter Cade/Tony Stone Images; B48 (b) Fred Bavendain/Peter Arnold, Inc.; B48 (t) Tony Freeman/Photo Edit; B49 (b) Robert Frerck/Odyssey Productions; B49 (t) Russell D. Curtis/Photo Researchers; B50 Wendell Metzen/Bruce Coleman; B51 Norman Owen Romalin/Bruce Coleman; B53 Laima Druskis/Photo Researchers; B54 Renee Lynn/Photo Researchers; B55 (r) Bernd Wittich/Visuals Unlimited; B56 Richard Hutchings/Picture It; B57 Don Riepe/Peter Arnold, Inc.; B58 (t) Andrew Rakoczy/Bruce Coleman Inc.; B59 (t) Grant Heilman; B60 (1) Robert Frerek/Odyssey Productions; B60 (2) John M. Roberts /The Stock Market; B60 (3) Laima Druskis/Photo Researchers; B60 (4) John Eastcott/Yva Momatiuk/Stock, Boston; B60 (5) Jim Corwin/Stone; B60 (b) Brian Parker/Tom Stack & Associates; B60 (c) Michael Groen Photography; B60 (d) Norman Owen Tomalin/Bruce Coleman, Inc.; B61 Bill Beatty/Visuals Unlimited; B64 Robert P. Falls Sr.

Unit C: C1 Into The Wind; (bg) Simon Fraser/SPLPhoto Researchers; C2-3 David Ball/The Stock Market; C3 (l) Dan Logen/Visuals Unlimited; C5 Lee Foster/Bruce Coleman Inc.; C6 (b) David Ball/The Stock Market; C6 (cb) N. P. Alexander/Visuals Unlimited; C6 (ct) Michael Groen Photography; C6-C7 (t) Tom Bean Tom Bean Photography; C7 (c) Uniphoto; C7 (l) Bill Everitt/Tom Stack & Associates; C9 Callaway Gardens, Georgia; C10 (b) Michael Groen Photography; C10 (t) Michael Lisnet/Gamma Liaison International; C11 (b) Don & Pat Valenti/DRK; C11 (c) Michael Groen Photography; C11 (t) Jonathan Rehg/Gamma Liaison International; C12 (bc) Daniel Heuclin; C12 (tl) Bill Barksdale/AGStock USA; C13 (br) David R. Frazier/Photo Researchers;

C15 (bl) Alese/Mort Pechter/The Stock Market; C15 (r) Stephen Ogilvy/Picture It; C15 (tl) Uniphoto; C16 (b) David Madison/Stone; C16 (c) Tom Dee, Ann McCarthy/The Stock Market; C16 (t) Stephen Ogilvy/Picture It; C17 (b) Jeff Greenberg/Photo Edit; Cl7 (r) Seth Goltzer/The Stock Market; C18 (cc) Stephen Frisch/Stock Boston; C18 (lc) Ed Malitsky/Gamma Liaison International; C18 (r) David Madison/Stone; C18(t) Lawrence Migdale/Stock Boston; C19(t) Tomas Muscionico/Contact Press Images; C19 (c) Tim Thayer/Gagosian Gallery; C20 (b) Pete Seaward/Stone; C20 (c) Andrew J. Martinez/Photo Researchers, Inc.; C25 John Cancalosi/Peter Arnold, Inc.; C26-27 John Cancalosi/Peter Arnold, Inc.; C27 (br) R.T. Nowitz/Nowitz Photos; C28 (b) John Cancalosi/Stock Boston; C28 (c) David Schwimmer/Bruce Coleman Inc.; C28 (t) David I. Sams/Stone; C29 (b) Peter Menzel/Stock Boston; C29 (c) Earl Scott/Photo Researchers, Inc.; C29 (t) E.R. Degginger/Bruce Coleman Inc.; C31 Les Stone/Sygma; C32(l) David R. Frazier/Photo Researchers, Inc.; C32 (r) Rich Frishman/Stone; C33 (b) Patrick Aventurier/Gamma-Liaison International; C33 (t) D.B. Dutheil/Sygma; C34(t) Tui De Roy/Minden Pictures; C34-35 (b) Francois Fohier/Photo Researchers; C35 (rc) Courtesy Dept. of Library Services, Americna Museum of Natural History, photo by Chip Clark; C35 (t) Renee Lynn/Photo Researchers; C37 Mark Perlstein/Black Star; C38-39 (b) C. Chesek & D. Finnin/American Museum of Natural History; C39 (t) The Royal Tyrrell Museum Library; C40 (bl) A.J. Copley/Visuals Unlimited; C40 Bruce Selyem Photo/Museum of the Rockies; C41 (b) Linda J. Moore; C41 (t) Francois Gohier/Photo Researchers, Inc.; C43 (b) Stephen Ogilvy/Picture It; C43-C44 (b) Louis Psihoyos/Matrix; C45 David M. Dennis/Tom Stack & Associates; C48 The Academy of Natural Sciences, Philadelphia.

Unit D: D2-D3 NASA/The Stock Market; D3 Uniphoto; D5 (bg) Jeff Adamo/The Stock Market; D5 (fg) Stephen Frisch/Stock Boston; D6 (b) Celestial Image Picture Co./Science Photo Library/Photo Researchers; D6-D7(t) Jerry Schad/Photo Researchers, Inc.; D7 (b) Stephen Ogilvy/Picture It; D8 Jerry Schad/Photo Researchers, Inc. D9 John Sanford/Photo Researchers. Inc.; D13 C.C. Lockwood/Animals Animals/Earth Scenes; D14-D15 (b) Ron Dahlquist/Stone; D15 (c) Clyde H. Smith/Peter Arnold, Inc.; D15 (t) NASA/Science Source/Photo Researchers, Inc.; D16 Jose Fuste Raga/The Stock Market; D17 Jeff Greenberg/Visuals Unlimited; D22-23 Mug Shots/The Stock Market; D25 Scott Nielsen/Bruce Coleman Inc.; D26-27 (bg) Dan McCoy/The Stock Market; D27 NASA/Peter Arnold, Inc.; D28-29 John Sanford/Science Photo Library/Photo Researchers, Inc.; D31-D32 (t) Jerry Schad/Photo Researchers, Inc.; D32 (t) John Stafford/Science Photo Library/Photo Researchers, Inc.; D34-35 Daniele Pellegrini/Photo Researchers, Inc.; D35 Tui de Roy/Minden Pictures; D37 (t) B. Yarvin/Image Works; D38 (b) Myrleen Cate/Stone; D38 (t) Mark S. Skalny/Visuals Unlimited; D39 (b) Michael Black/Bruce Coleman Inc.; D39 (t) W. Scarberry/ Image Works; D40 (b) Momatiuk/Eastcott/Image Works; D40 (t) Charles Feil/Stock, Boston; D41 (b) David R. Frazier; D41 (r) Lawrence Migdale/Photo Researchers, Inc.; D43 Martin Bond/Science Photo Library/Photo Researchers, Inc.; D47 Cape Grim B.A.P.S./Simon Fraser/Science Library/Photo Researchers, Inc.; D48 (lc) Michael Groen Photography; D48-D49 (l)Stuart Craig, Jr./Bruce Coleman Inc.; D49 (r) David Parker/Science Photo Library/Photo Researchers, Inc.; D49 (t) Richard Hutchings/Picture It; D50 (b) Trevor Mein/Stone; D50-D51 (c) John Shaw/Bruce Coleman Inc.; D50-D51 (t) David Woods/The Stock Market; D58 (b) Michael Groen Photography; D58 (t) Mark Perlstein/Black Star; D59 (t) Jean F. Stoick/Peter Arnold, Inc.; D60 (tl) Peter Miller/Photo Researchers, Inc.; D60 (tlc) David Pollack/The Stock Market; D60 (trc) Kent Wood/Photo Researchers; D60 (tr) Larry Miller/ Photo Researchers, Inc.; D64 Joseph Nettis/Photo Researchers, Inc.

Unit E: E2-E3 G. Brad Lewis/Gamma-Liaison International; E5 Stephen Ogilvy/Picture It; E6 Michael Groen Photography; E6-E7 (tl) Stephen Ogilvy/Picture It; E9 Richard Hutchings/Picture It; E10-E11 Michael Groen Photography; E12-E13 (r) Stephen Ogilvy/Picture It; E16-E17 Michael Groen Photography; E18-19 Stephen Ogilvy/Picture It; E21 Joseph Sohm/The Stock Market; E22 (l) Pat Lanza/Bruce Coleman Inc.; E22 (r) Stephen Ogilvy/Picture It; E23 (br) Richard Hutchings/Photo Researchers. Inc.; E23 (r) Richard Hutchings/Picture It; E23 (t) Royce Bair/Uniphoto; E24-E25 (l) Stephen Ogilvy/Picture It; E25 (br) Michael Groen Photography; E25 (t) U.S. Dept. of Transportation; E27 (t) Michael Groen Photography; E28 (tl, tc, 4, 5, 6, 7) Michael Groen Photography; E28-E29 (r, 2, 3) Stephen Ogilvy/Picture It; E30-E31 Scott T. Smith/The Stock Solution; E31 Arlene L. Parnes/Photo Researchers, Inc.; E32-33 Bryan F. Peterson/The Stock Market; E33 Michael Groen Photography; E34-37 Michael Groen Photography; E39 Giovanni Simeone/The Stock Market; E42 (b) Bob Llewellyn/Uniphoto; E42 (t) S. Dooley/Gamma Liaison International; E43 (b) Michael DeYoung/Uniphoto; E43 (t) W. A. Banaszewski/Visuals Unlimited; E45 Michael Groen Photography; E46 Stephen Ogilvy/Picture It; E46 (b) Michael Groen Photography; E47 Stephen Ogilvy/Picture It; E48 Barbara Leslie/FPG International; E49 Michael Groen Photography; E51(l) Martha Cooper/Peter Arnold, Inc.; E52 (t) George Mattei/Envision; E52 (c) Michael Groen Photography; E52 (tc) Aaron Haupt/Stock, Boston; E52 (tl) Michael Groen Photography; E52 (tr) Barbara Leslie/FPG International; E56 Robert C. Williams/American Museum of Papermaking.

Unit F: F2-F3 Laguna Photo/Gamma-Liaison International; F3 Brian Parker/Tom Stack & Associates; F6 (bl) Stephen Ogilvy/Picture It; F6 (tl) David R. Frazier/Photo Researchers, Inc.; F7 (t) Stephen Ogilvy/Picture It; F10 (b) Richard Pasley/Stock Boston; F10 (t) Don Kreuter/Rainbow; F11 (b) Stephen Ogilvy/Picture It; F11 (t) MacDonald Photography/Unicorn Stock Photos; F19 Frank Pennington/Unicorn Stock Photos; F20 (tr) Richard Pasley/Stock Boston; F20-21 (b) Richard Hutchings/Picture It; F22 (b) Jim Cummins/FPG International; F26 (a) B. Daemmrich/Image Works; F26 (b) Jim Cummins/FPG International; F26 (b) MacDonald Photography/Unicorn Stock Photos; F26 (r) Frank Pennington/Unicorn Stock Photos; F26 (t) Phil Jason/Stone; F28 Tim Davis/Stone; F29 (l) James H. Robinson/Photo Researchers, Inc.; F31 A. Ramey/Photo Edit; F32 (r) Richard Hutchings/Photo Edit; F33 (b) Spencer Grant/Photo Edit; F33 (t) Michael Groen Photography; F34-35 (l) Stephen Ogilvy/ Picture It; F37 Ken Graham/Bruce Coleman Inc.; F38 Stephen Ogilvy/Picture It; F39 (b) Stephen J. Krasemann/DRK Photo; F39 (t) Barbara Gerlach/DRK Photo; F41 Stacy Pick/Stock, Boston; F42 (t) Stephen Ogilvy/Picture It; F44 Stuart Westmoreland/Stone; F44-45 Amos Nachoum/The Stock Market; F47 Eric Freedman/Bruce Coleman Inc.; F51 (c) Doug Martin/Photo Researchers, Inc.; F51 (r) Doug Martin/PhotoEdit; F51 (c) Doug Martin/Photo Researchers, Inc.; F52 (2) A. Ramey/PhotoEdit; F52 (3l) Renee Lynn/Photo Researchers, Inc.; F52 (3r) Robert Haddock/Stone; F52 (a) Stephen J. Krasemann/DRK Photo; F52 (b) Stuart Westmoreland/Stone; F56 Jeff Greenberg/Photo Researchers, Inc.

All other photographs by Harcourt School Publishers, © Harcourt.

Illustration Credits: Kate Sweeney A49, A50, A51, A52, A55, A56, A57, A58, A61, A62, A63; Steven Stankiewicz A68; Patrick Gnan B36; Malcom Ellis C23; Susan Carlson C26-27; Margarita Cruz C38-39; Jon Weiman C42; Sue Carlson C44; Wendy Smith C45; Christer Eriksson D16, D17, D19, D20-21, D22-23; Rachel Geswaldo (electronic art) D30; Tim Haggerty E2; Lori Anzalone E40; Gary Ciccarelli E41; Rachel Geswaldo (electronic art) F7; Kate Sweeney F34.